Richard D. Brecht, Cynthia Martin

RUSSIAN

stage two
American Edition

Grammar for Communication:
Analysis and Commentaries

Series Editor: Dan E. Davidson

American Council of Teachers of Russian
1776 Massachusetts Ave., NW Washington DC 20036

KENDALL/HUNT PUBLISHING COMPANY
4050 Westmark Drive   Dubuque, Iowa 52002

CREDITS

Edited by:
Maria Lekic

Design and Cover by:
Tatiana Zagorskaya

Preface

Russian Stage Two: American Edition is part of the series that includes *Live from Moscow!: Russian Stage One* and *Russian Stage Three: Focus on Speaking.* The goal of *Russian Stage Two* is to help students attain solid intermediate-level speaking proficiency based on the activization of the essentials of Russian grammar encountered in a beginning course of study. The major grammatical topics treated in *Russian Stage Two* are generated by the contexts of the communicative themes forming the basis of each unit. Hence, this new Grammar Commentaries is intended not as a comprehensive grammar, but rather as a set of functional explanations that place the situationally motivated material of each unit into its grammatical context.

The ten units of the Grammar Commentaries correspond to each of the ten units of the main textbook, and are titled accordingly. The shadowboxes from the units are replicated here to facilitate cross-referencing. References to other units in the textbook and to the Appendicies are included as appropriate, as well. Provided that students have successfully completed an introductory course before beginning *Russian Stage Two,* no other sources of grammatical explanations will be required at this level of study. The *Supplemental Grammar Keys* by Nathan Longan that accompany *Russian Stage Two* provide translations and grammar pointers on an exercise-by-exercise basis for materials contained in the main textbook, as well as answer keys for most of the exercises in the workbook.

Acknowledgements

The authors wish to acknowledge the invaluable contributions of all those who participated in the development of these *Commentaries*. We are particularly grateful to Dr. Maria Lekic, Director of Materials Development and Publications at the American Council of Teachers of Russian and Professor of Russian at the University of Maryland, for her professional insight and support of the project. A special thanks goes to Dan Davidson, Executive Director of ACTR/ACCELS and Professor of Russian and Second Language Acquisition at Bryn Mawr College, who through the years has been an active and creative participant in the exploration of the grammatical domains of Russian. We are grateful to Dr. Kira Gor of the University of Maryland for her assistance and suggestions for the improvement of the materials. A special note of gratitude goes to Jennifer Gregory of ACTR for her conscientious editing, both substantive and technical. We also wish to thank Irina Van Dusen of the Washington D.C. based staff of ACTR for her efforts. Finally, we wish to extend a special note of thanks to all the teachers and students of Russian who have used *Russian Stage Two* in the past and whose experience and suggestions have helped to define this project. The authors welcome suggestions for the continued improvement of these materials in the future.

Our appreciation is also extended to the institutions that have supported this project and its authors: the American Council of Teachers of Russian, the University of Maryland, College Park, and the National Foreign Language Center, Washington, D.C.

Содержа́ние

Preface i
Acknowledgements...iii

Уро́к 1: Дава́йте познако́мимся!   1

1. Making someone's acquaintance *1*
2. The absence of the verb "to be" in the present tense: review *2*
3. Verbs of studying and learning *3*
4. Discussing professions *6*
5. Expressing location: review *7*
6. Expressing possession: review *8*
7. Review of impersonal or "subjectless" sentences *11*
8. Reported speech *14*
9. Note on verbal adverbs and adjectives (participles) for reading *16*

Уро́к 2: Ка́к прое́хать? Как пройти́?   17

1. Spatial prepositions and their complements *17*
2. Verbs of motion: overview *18*
3. Review of unprefixed verbs of motion *19*
4. Carrying and transporting: transitive verbs of motion *24*
5. Prefixed verbs of motion *25*

Уро́к 3: Когда́? Во ско́лько? На ско́лько?   35

1. Expressing clock time in Russian *35*
2. Time when: days, weeks, months and seasons *39*
3. The prepositions на and через in time expressions *42*
4. The prepositions за... до... to express time elapsing before an action *43*
5. Expressing duration *44*
6. Не́когда *46*
7. Simultaneous vs. sequential actions and aspect *46*
8. Imperfective or perfective infinitive after certain verbs *48*

9. Verbs with the particle -ся (-сь): reflexive meaning *49*
10. The conjunctions после того́, как; до того́, как; and перед те́м, как *50*
11. Common short-form adjectives *51*
12. The emphatic pronoun са́м, сама́, само́ *52*

Уро́к 4: Ка́к о́н (она́) вы́глядит? В чём о́н (она́)? 55

1. Describing personal appearance *55*
2. The verb нра́виться/понра́виться *59*
3. He + imperfective infinitive *59*
4. Aspect and annulled action *60*
5. The emphatic pronoun са́м, сама́, са́ми *62*
6. The verbs спра́шивать/спроси́ть and проси́ть/попроси́ть *62*

Уро́к 5: Где мо́жно купи́ть...? 65

1. More verbs with the particle -ся *65*
2. Simple comparative of adjectives and adverbs *66*
3. Second-person imperative: review *71*
4. Aspect and the modal word нельзя́ *76*
5. Review of double negation rule *77*

Уро́к 6: Прия́тного аппети́та! 79

1. Verbs of position and positioning *79*
2. Case usage and verbs after numbers *81*
3. Instrumental case in definitions and descriptions *83*
4. The indefinite particles -то and -нибудь *84*
5. First-person imperative: "Let's...!" *86*
6. Third-person imperative *87*
7. Пора́ *87*
8. Expressing a plural subject *88*
9. Review of relative clauses: кото́рый *89*
10. Verbal adjectives (participles) for reading *90*

Урóк 7: Бы́ли ли вы́ на премьéре? 97

1. The preposition по *97*
2. Expressing a round trip in past or future: the perfective verbs сходи́ть and съéздить *99*
3. Subordinate clauses with котóрый *101*
4. Довóлен, довóльна, довóльны (чéм): to be pleased/satisfied with *102*
5. Overview of verbs of studying, learning and teaching *103*
6. The superlative degree of adjectives and adverbs *107*
7. Passive constructions using short-form verbal adjectives (participles) *109*
8. Summary and review: long- and short-form adjectives *112*

Урóк 8: Кáк вы себя́ чу́вствуете? 121

1. Discussing health *121*
2. Describing the weather *124*
3. Simultaneous vs. consecutive actions and aspect *126*
4. The conjunctions поэ́тому and потому́ что *127*
5. Clauses of purpose introduced by чтобы *128*
6. "If... then...." clauses expressing real conditions *128*
7. The subjunctive mood *129*

Урóк 9: Чéм вы́ увлекáетесь? Чтó вáс интересу́ет? 131

1. Expressing interests: занимáться, увлекáться, интересовáться *131*
2. Multi-directional verbs of motion to describe a general activity *132*
3. Imperfective infinitives after certain verbs *133*
4. The construction оди́н из + genitive case *135*
5. Describing activities and sports events *135*
6. Transitive vs. intransitive reflexive verbs: уви́деть/уви́деться, встрéтить/встрéтиться, познакóмить/познакóмиться *137*

Уро́к 10: Мы́ путеше́ствуем!   139

1. Multidirectional verbs of motion in the past to indicate round trip   *139*
2. По + dative to indicate motion all around   *139*
3. Short-form adjectives дово́лен (дово́льна, дово́льны) and ви́ден (видна́, ви́дно, видны́)   *140*
4. Expressing one's impressions   *140*
5. Means of transportation   *142*
6. Prefixes с-, по-, and про-, and multidirectional verbs of motion   *142*
7. Verbal adverbs (gerunds)   *145*

Уро́к 1: Дава́йте познако́мимся!

1. Making someone's acquaintance

> Дава́йте познако́мимся. Меня́ зову́т Джон.
> Let me introduce myself. My name is John.

A. Ка́к ва́с зову́т?

To state or ask for a person's name, use the following formula.

> зову́т[1] + *accusative case of noun or pronoun denoting the person*

— Ка́к ва́с зову́т?   "What is your name?"
— Меня́ зову́т Ли́нда.   "My name is Linda."

— Ка́к зову́т э́ту де́вушку? "What is that girl's name?"
— Её зову́т Ната́ша.   "Her name is Natasha."

— Ка́к зову́т э́того челове́ка? "What is that man's name?"
— Его́ зову́т Джон.   "His name is John."

B. Introductions

To introduce yourself, use the first-person imperative.

— Дава́йте познако́мимся! "Let me introduce myself."
           Lit.: "Let's get acquainted."

The following is a more formal way to introduce yourself.

---

[1] Зову́т is the third-person plural form of зва́ть (з/ва^{x}-) "call."

Разреши́те предста́виться.	Permit me to introduce myself.

Use the second-person imperative to introduce two parties to one another.

— Познако́мьтесь, пожа́луйста.	"Let me introduce you." *Lit.: "Please get acquainted."*

2. The absence of the verb "to be" in the present tense: review

Э́то Ната́ша. Она́ моя́ сосе́дка. Она́ студе́нтка.
This is Natasha. She is my neighbor. She is a student.

Её специа́льность — микробиоло́гия.
She is a microbiology major.

Джо́н америка́нец.
John is an American.

Unlike English, in Russian there is no present tense of the verb "to be" (**бы́ть**) linking the subject and the predicate in equational sentences.

Я Ли́нда. = I *am* Linda.

Sentences of this type are common in unit one, which focuses on providing and soliciting information about new people and places. Here are some examples.

Э́то Ната́ша.	This is Natasha.
Э́то на́ш университе́т.	This is our university.
Э́то страхово́е аге́нство.	This is an insurance company.
Она́ студе́нтка.	She is a student.

Джóн америкáнец.	John is an American.
Онá психóлог.	She is a psychologist.
Мы́ друзья́.	We are friends.
Онá моя́ сосéдка.	She is my neighbor (*or:* roommate).
Егó специáльность — рýсский язы́к.	He is majoring in Russian.
Олéг прекрáсный специалíст.	Oleg is an excellent specialist.
Мóй гóрод красíвый.	My city is beautiful.
Нáша машíна нóвая.	Our car is new.

3. Verbs of studying and learning

Джóн ýчится в университéте.

John goes to college.

Он занимáется совремéнной эконóмикой Россíи.

He is studying contemporary Russian economics.

Because of their diversity and high frequency, verbs pertaining to teaching, studying, and learning deserve special attention. The verbs listed below appear in this unit. Other verbs of studying will be discussed later in the book[1].

A. Занимáться чéм: "study," "be occupied with," "major in"

This intransitive[2] verb denotes participation in a wide range of academic, vocational, and avocational pursuits. It is the usual way of conveying the idea of "majoring" at the undergraduate level. Its complement is in the instrumental case.

---

[1] For a complete review of verbs pertaining to studying, learning, and teaching, see *Unit 7, #5*.

[2] An intransitive verb is one that does not take a direct object. All verbs ending in the particle **-ся (-сь)** are intransitive.

Джо́н занима́ется совреме́нной эконо́микой Росси́и.	He is studying/majoring in contemporary Russian economics.
Мы́ занима́емся ру́сским языко́м.	We are studying/majoring in Russian.
Ива́н занима́ется междунаро́дным би́знесом.	Ivan is studying/majoring in international business.
Ле́сли занима́ется марке́тингом.	Leslie is studying/majoring in marketing.

When used without a complement, **занима́ться** means to prepare for class (e.g. by reading class assignments, taking notes, doing homework.)

Ли́нда занима́ется.	Linda is studying. *(Studying as opposed to, for example, relaxing or working.)*

B. Учи́ться где́: "to study" (in the sense of "to be a student");
intransitive; imperfective only

> Джо́н у́чится в университе́те на второ́м ку́рсе.
> John is a sophomore in college.

The verb **учи́ться** indicates matriculation in a school, college, university, or other program of study.

Мы́ у́чимся в Мэриле́ндском университе́те.	We go to the University of Maryland.
Они́ у́чатся в шко́ле би́знеса.	He is going to business school.

Ма́ша у́чится на компью́терных ку́рсах.	Masha is taking computer classes.

C. Учи́ть/вы́учить что́: "to learn, memorize"

Ли́нда у́чит ру́сский язы́к уже́ го́д.	Linda has been learning Russian for an entire year.
В шко́ле де́ти у́чат матема́тику и геогра́фию.	Children learn mathematics and geography in school.

Учи́ть/вы́учить denotes learning by rote: learning words; memorizing a poem or a part in a play; or studying lesson materials, rules, and discrete data (as, for example, for an examination). This verb is rarely used without an object[1].

Мы́ вы́учили все́ но́вые слова́.	We learned/memorized all of the new words.

D. "Student"

The English word "student" is very versatile and can refer to a variety of learners. In contrast, the equivalent Russian terms are much more specific.

- **Студе́нт/студе́нтка** refer only to college students.
- **Аспира́нт/аспира́нтка** refer to graduate students.
- **Шко́льник/шко́льница** and **учени́к/учени́ца** refer to pupils in elementary through high school.

---

[1] In answer to the general question, «Что́ ты́ де́лаешь?» you can say «Я занима́юсь», but NOT «Я учу́».

4. Discussing professions

Study the variety of constructions used in *Unit 1* for discussing one's profession.

Ктó вы́?	What do you do (for a living)?
— Ктó ва́ш бра́т? — Мóй бра́т — программи́ст.	"What does your brother do (for a — living)?" "My brother is a computer programmer."
Ната́ша консульта́нт по маркéтингу.	Natasha is a marketing consultant.

По профéссии + the name of the profession means "By profession s/he is...."

— Ктó ва́ш бра́т по профéссии? — Он по профéссии программи́ст.	"What is your brother's profession?" "He is a computer programmer by profession."

You can use **специали́ст по** + dative to say, "S/he specializes in...."

Тóм адвока́т. Он специали́ст пó междунарóдному пра́ву.
Tom is a lawyer. He specializes in international law.

Лéна психóлог. Она́ специали́ст пó дéтской психолóгии.
Lena is a psychologist. She specializes in child psychology.

Специа́льность (*f.*) can mean either one's "major" or one's professional expertise within a broader field.

—Кака́я у ва́с специа́льность в университе́те?
—У меня́ специа́льность — ру́сский язы́к.
"What is your major at the university?"
"My major is Russian."

Его́ специа́льность — програми́рование.
His field of expertise is programming.

Её специа́льность — марке́тинг.
Her field of expertise is marketing.

Рабо́тать ке́м means, "to work as a...."

Ната́ша рабо́тает официа́нткой.
Natasha works as (is) a waitress.

Моя́ ма́ма рабо́тает дире́ктором шко́лы.
My mother works as (is) the principal of a school.

Мо́й оте́ц рабо́тал инжене́ром.
My father used to work as (was) an engineer.

5. Expressing location: review

Expressions of location are used frequently throughout *Unit 1*. Many verbs used to describe people, such as **роди́ться, жи́ть, рабо́тать,** and **учи́ться,** are followed by location.

If a noun expressing location denotes a person, it is used in the genitive form with the preposition **у**; all other nouns are used in the prepositional case with **в** or **на**. The group of nouns that require **на**, commonly referred to as "**на**-nouns," must be memorized[1].

---

[1] See *Appendix VIII* for a list of **на**-nouns.

Гдé?

<table>
<tr><td colspan="3">в (+prepositional)</td></tr>
<tr><td>в гóроде</td><td>в шкóле</td><td>в магазúнах</td></tr>
<tr><td>in the city</td><td>at school</td><td>in stores</td></tr>
</table>

<table>
<tr><td colspan="3">на (+prepositional)</td></tr>
<tr><td>на вы́ставке</td><td>на Урáле</td><td>на кýрсах</td></tr>
<tr><td>at the exhibit</td><td>in the Urals</td><td>in classes</td></tr>
</table>

<table>
<tr><td colspan="3">у (+genitive)</td></tr>
<tr><td>у брáта</td><td>у сестры́</td><td>у родúтелей</td></tr>
<tr><td>at (one's)
brother's</td><td>at (one's)
sister's</td><td>at (one's)
parents'</td></tr>
</table>

Remember that when **на** is used with nouns that normally take **в** to indicate location, it means "on top of," "on the surface of."

6. Expressing possession: review

У негó éсть друзья́.

He has friends.

У негó нéт друзéй.

He doesn't have any friends.

У негó мнóго друзéй.

He has a lot of friends.

The following is a brief review of constructions of possession.

A. Expressing possession: éсть

The present tense of the verb **éсть** is used to establish possession. **Есть** does not change to agree with the subject.

The preposition **y** + the genitive case is used to indicate possession by a *person*.

— У тебя́ éсть компью́тер?	"Do you have a computer?"
— Да́, у меня́ éсть компью́тер. Он но́вый.	"Yes, I have a computer. It's new."
— У ва́с éсть ко́шка и́ли соба́ка?	"Do you have a cat or a dog?"
— Да́, у на́с éсть ко́шка и соба́ка.	"Yes, we have a cat and a dog."

Есть is omitted when the emphasis is on anything other than the *fact of possession;* e.g., on the *quality* or *quantity* of the item.

У на́с éсть маши́на. We have a car.	*Statement of possession of a car.*
У на́с но́вая, хоро́шая маши́на. We have a nice, new car.	*Statement of possession, with emphasis on the quality of the car—it is nice and new—rather than on the mere possession of the item.*
У на́с две́ маши́ны. We have two cars.	*Statement of possession, with emphasis on the quantity of the item.*

Recall that the past and future tenses of **éсть** are the same as they are for the verb **бы́ть**, and agree in number and gender with the object possessed (which is in the nominative case in Russian).

У меня́ была́ маши́на.	I used to have a car.
У меня́ бы́л компью́тер, но́ я его́ про́дал.	I had a computer, but I sold it.
У меня́ бу́дет маши́на.	I will have a car.
У на́с бу́дут де́ньги.	We will have money.

B. Denying possession: нéт

Нéт + the genitive case is used to deny possession or express the absence of an item.

У меня́ нéт сестры́.	I don't have a sister.
У нáс нéт кóшки.	We don't have a cat.
У меня́ нéт компью́тера.	I don't have a computer.
У меня́ нéт дéнег.	I don't have any money.

In the past and future, absence is expressed using the third-person neuter singular form of **éсть** (**бы́ло** or **бýдет**) + genitive, regardless of the gender and number of the item in question. Remember that in the past tense, the stress falls on the **нé** and **нé было** is pronounced as a single unit.

У меня́ нé было компью́тера.
I didn't have a computer.

У меня́ не бýдет компью́тера.
I won't have a computer.

У ни́х нé было маши́ны.
They didn't have a car.

У ни́х не бýдет маши́ны.
They won't have a car.

У нáс нé было дéнег.
We didn't have any money.

У нáс не бýдет дéнег.
We won't have any money.

"Neither... nor...." is expressed in Russian by **ни..., ни....** + the genitive case in a negative sentence.

У меня́ нéт ни сестры́, ни брáта.
I don't have a brother or a sister. (I have neither a brother nor a sister.)

У меня́ нéт ни бумáги, ни рýчки.
I don't have either paper or a pen. (I have neither paper nor a pen.)

Note also the adjective **никакóй** used as an intensifier meaning, "none at all."

У меня́ нéт никакúх дéнег.   I don't have any money at all.

7. Review of impersonal or "subjectless" sentences

While every English sentence must have a grammatical subject, Russian sentences without a subject are quite common. The word "subject" in this case refers to a noun or pronoun in the nominative case with which the predicate agrees in person, gender, and number. Here are some examples of sentences with grammatical subjects.

Сергéй смешнóй.   Sergey is funny.

Джóн интерéсный человéк.   John is an interesting person.

Натáша óчень ýмная.   Natasha is very smart.

Нáше общежúтие нóвое.   Our dormitory is new.

Impersonal sentences are "subjectless" because they contain only one main part of the sentence: the predicate. The predicate is always in the *neuter singular* and can take the form of an impersonal verb (or a personal verb used impersonally), an adverb, or a short-form adjective.

In this unit, impersonal sentences are used to describe emotional states, attitudes, and physical conditions that are not attributable to a particular person. The predicate is an adverb or a short-form adjective in the *neuter singular* (ending in **-o**).

Хóлодно.   It's cold.

When the person experiencing the state or emotion[1] is mentioned, the noun or pronoun denoting that person is in the *dative case*.

Мнé хóлодно.   I'm cold.

---

[1] This person is sometimes referred to as the "logical subject."

Compare:

Су́п холо́дный.

Ива́ну хо́лодно.

The first sentence describes the *physical condition* of the soup; the second characterizes the physical state Ivan *is experiencing* independent of his own volition.

Compare the following pairs of personal and impersonal sentences.

Он плохо́й.	He is bad.
Ему́ пло́хо.	He doesn't feel well.
Ле́кция была́ интере́сная.	The lecture was interesting.
На ле́кции мне́ бы́ло интере́сно.	It was interesting (for me) at the lecture.
На́ш до́м тёплый.	Our building is warm. (i.e., well-insulated)
Зде́сь на́м тепло́.	We are warm here.
Кре́сло удо́бное.	This armchair is comfortable.
Мне́ удо́бно в кре́сле.	I am comfortable in this armchair.
Экза́мен бы́л тру́дный.	The exam was hard.
На экза́мене мне́ бы́ло тру́дно.	It was difficult at the exam. (i.e., I struggled during the exam.)
Э́тот фи́льм гру́стный.	That film is sad.
Мне́ бы́ло гру́стно (по́сле фи́льма).	I was (felt) sad after the film.
Джо́н смешно́й челове́к.	John is a funny person.
Джо́ну бы́ло смешно́ на спекта́кле.	It was funny at the show (to John).

Note that in sentences with grammatical subjects (the first in each pair), the predicate verb **быть** agrees with the subject in the past and future tense. In the second sentence of each set, the predicate verb **быть** has no grammatical subject to agree with, and thus is always in the *neuter singular* in the past and future tenses.

Impersonal statements are used to express one's attitude to a situation as a whole.

Мне́ интере́сно.	It's/this is interesting (for me).

Again, if the person experiencing the state or providing the assessment is given, the noun or pronoun denoting that person is in the dative case.

Мне́ удо́бно.	I'm comfortable.
Ей всё равно́.	She doesn't care.
На́м сло́жно.	It's hard for us.
Ната́ше бы́ло ску́чно.	Natasha was bored.
Серге́ю бу́дет ве́село.	Sergey will have a good time.

It is impossible to render many of these impersonal statements into English without using "it," "that," or "this" as the "subject." In Russian, it is possible to use *just the predicate* in expressing one's attitude toward a situation.

— Ка́к бы́ло на вы́ставке?	"How was it at the exhibit?"
— Интере́сно. (Интере́сно бы́ло.)	"It was interesting."
— Пойдём с на́ми к Ната́ше.	"Go with us to Natasha's."
— Неудо́бно бу́дет.	"That would be awkward."
— Ка́к бы́ло у Лёны?	"How was it at Lena's?"
— О́чень ве́село (бы́ло).	"It was really fun."

— Ка́к сейча́с на у́лице?　　　　"What's it like outside?"
— На у́лице прия́тно.　　　　　"It's nice outside."

8. Reported speech

In each unit of *Russian: Stage Two*, there are exercises requiring you to render direct speech as reported speech. To do so, you must know the following rules[1].

A. Reported statements

Preserve the tense of the verb in the original utterance, regardless of what the English equivalent requires.

Он сказа́л: «Я живу́ с роди́телями».　　He said, "I live with my parents."

Он сказа́л, что́ о́н живёт с роди́телями.　　He said that he lived (lives) with his parents.

Ната́ша сказа́ла: «Я бу́ду учи́ться в университе́те».　　Natasha said, "I'm going to go to college."

Ната́ша сказа́ла, что она́ бу́дет учи́ться в университе́те.　　Natasha said that she was going (is going) to go to college.

B. Reported Questions

1. For a question with an interrogative ("question") word, preserve the tense of the original utterance.

Ли́нда спроси́ла Са́шу: «Че́м вы́ занима́етесь?»　　Linda asked Sasha, "What are you studying?"

---

[1] Note the consistent use of the comma before the reported clause in the second example of each pair.

Ли́нда спроси́ла Са́шу, чём о́н занима́ется.	Linda asked Sasha what he was studying.
Он спроси́л: «Где́ ты́ рабо́таешь?»	He asked, "Where do you work?"
Он спроси́л, где́ я́ рабо́таю.	He asked where I work.

2. For a yes/no question, preserve the tense of the original utterance and use the following construction.

predicate + **ли** + *subject*

Она́ спроси́ла меня́: «Вы́ говори́те по-англи́йски?»	She asked me, "Do you speak English?"
Она́ спроси́ла меня́, говорю́ ли я́ по-англи́йски.	She asked me whether I speak English.

Note how questions that include a choice are reported.

Она́ спроси́ла: «Ты́ у́чишься и́ли рабо́таешь?»	She asked, "Do you go to school or work?"
Она́ спроси́ла, учу́сь ли я́ и́ли рабо́таю.	She asked whether I go to school or work.

C. Reported commands, requests, wishes

Use **что́бы** + the past tense of the verb.

Он сказа́л мне́: «Позвони́ Джо́ну ве́чером.»	He told me, "Call John this evening."

Он сказáл мнé, чтóбы я́ позвонúла Джóну вéчером.	He told me to call John this evening.

Note how a statement with a first-person imperative can be reported.

Джóн сказáл: «Давáйте пойдём в кинó».	John said, "Let's go to the movies."
Джóн предложúл пойтú в кинó.	John suggested that we go to the movies.

9. Note on verbal adverbs and adjectives (participles) for reading

Verbal adverbs and adjectives are included throughout *Russian: Stage Two* primarily in the reading sections of each unit. The goal at this stage of study is to acquire only a *passive knowledge* of these forms. These forms are noted in the commentary sections as encountered in the reading texts. A detailed analysis of participles is provided in *Unit 6* and of verbal adverbs in *Unit 10*. Beginning with *Unit 6*, homework assignments intended to help students recognize verbal adjective forms are included in each unit. Some practice with verbal adverbs is included in *Unit 10*.

Уро́к 2: Ка́к прое́хать? Ка́к пройти́?

1. Spatial prepositions and their complements

> Ци́рк нахо́дится недалеко́ от университе́та.
> The circus is not far from the university.

Memorize the following prepositions indicating location and their complements.

недалеко́ от + *gen.*	not far from, close to
сле́ва от + *gen.*	on the left of
спра́ва от + *gen.*	on the right of
за + *instr.*	behind
ря́дом с + *instr.*	next to
напро́тив + *gen.*	across from, opposite
ме́жду + *instr.*	between

2. Verbs of motion: overview

In Russian there are many verbs that indicate movement (e.g. **путеше́ствовать** "travel," **спеши́ть** "hurry," **дви́гаться** "move," etc.). However, there is a special group of 14 unprefixed pairs, the verbs of motion, that have *two imperfective forms*. Each of these two forms characterizes the direction of a movement in different ways. A unidirectional verb form signals that the movement proceeds in one direction, usually towards a stated or implied goal. A multidirectional verb is used when a movement has no definite direction, is repeated, or proceeds in several or many directions (i.e., is multidirectional).

3. Review of unprefixed verbs of motion

A. Forms

Russian: Stage Two covers the most important and widely used pairs of unprefixed verbs of motion. Their forms must be memorized[1]. Verbs that have an irregular conjugation are listed in boldface.

	Unidirectional Verb	*Multidirectional Verb*	*Definition*
Intransitive	**идти́**	ходи́ть	walk, go (on foot)
	éхать	éздить	go (by vehicle)
	плы́ть	пла́вать	swim, sail
	лете́ть	лета́ть	fly
	бежа́ть	бе́гать	run

Remember that all unprefixed uni- and multidirectional verbs are *imperfective* and conform to the general rules of aspect usage in Russian.

B. Main contexts for using unidirectional verbs

Unidirectional verbs are most often used to express an action as it advances along a given route, usually toward a specific destination. The following list describes the most common contexts in which unidirectional verbs are used.

1. Motion in one direction in progress

— Куда́ ты́ идёшь?   "Where are you going?"

— Я́ иду́ в магази́н за хле́бом.   "I'm going to the store to get bread."

---

[1] See *Appendix XIII* for full conjugations. Infinitive forms are used throughout the grammar commentaries. Stems are provided in all vocabulary lists for each unit, in the comprehensive dictionaries in the amin textbook, and in the appendices.

The clearest context requiring unidirectional verbs is that in which the action is seen *in progress* and *in one direction*. Thus, the question "Where are you going?" is rendered in Russian with a unidirectional verb: **«Куда́ вы́ идёте?»** (on foot) or **«Куда́ вы́ е́дете?»** (by vehicle). The answer, likewise, is rendered with a unidirectional verb: **«Мы́ идём (or е́дем) в теа́тр»**. Even if a destination is not mentioned, the unidirectional verb is still required if one is concentrating on an action taking place in one direction at the moment of speech. For example:

Someone on the bus asks a fellow passenger:

— Извини́те, я́ пра́вильно е́ду на Моско́вский вокза́л?
— Да́, вы́ пра́вильно е́дете. Московский вокза́л бу́дет через одну́ остано́вку.
"Am I going the right way to Moscow Station?"
"Yes, you're going the right way. Moscow Station will be the stop after next."

Two students who run into one another on campus:

— Куда́ ты́ спеши́шь?
— Я́ бегу́ в компью́терный це́нтр. Мне́ на́до зако́нчить свою́ рабо́ту.
"Where are you off to?"
"I'm running to the computer center. I have to finish my paper/project."

2. Circumstances surrounding the action of the main verb in complex sentences

Note that in the following complex sentences, a unidirectional verb of motion is used to indicate the circumstances surrounding the action described in the main clause. In all of the examples, the English "while on one's way" can be inserted.

Я встре́тил своего́ дру́га, когда́ я шёл на стадио́н.
I ran into my friend when I was on my way to the stadium.

Я вспо́мнила о собра́нии, когда́ я́ е́хала домо́й.
I remembered about the meeting on my way home.

Начался дождь, когда мы́ шли́ домо́й по́сле конце́рта.
It started raining when we were on our way home after the concert.

Когда́ я шла́ в библиоте́ку, я потеря́ла де́ньги.
On my way to the library, I lost the money.

3. Description of some aspect or quality of a unidirectional, one-time motion

Analyze the following examples of unidirectional verbs in which the speaker wishes to describe some aspect of the motion, such as the means of transportation, the speed, or the course of the motion; in other words, to answer the question, «*Ка́к е́хать? Ка́к идти́?*»

Мы́ е́хали в це́нтр на метро́, а они́ е́хали на маши́не.
We rode downtown on the metro, and they rode in a car. *(means of transportation)*

Обы́чно я́ хожу́ пешко́м в университе́т, но́ сего́дня я́ опозда́л(а) и е́хал(а) на авто́бусе. *(means of transportation)*
I usually walk to the university, but today I was late and rode the bus instead.

Мы́ прие́хали о́чень ра́но, Ива́н хорошо́ зна́ет го́род и мы́ е́хали о́чень бы́стро.
We arrived very early, Ivan knows the city well and we drove really fast.
(speed of one time, unidirectional motion)

— Скажи́те, кни́жный магази́н нахо́дится далеко́ отсю́да?
— Не́т, е́сли идти́ бы́стро, мо́жно дойти́ за де́сять мину́т.
"Tell me, is the bookstore far from here?"
"No, if you walk fast, you can get there in ten minutes." *(speed of one-time, unidirectional motion)*

4. Idiomatic Expressions

Unidirectional forms are also used in certain set expressions, in which various inanimate subjects are imagined to be in unidirectional motion.

Идёт до́ждь.	It's raining.
Вчера́ ве́сь де́нь шёл сне́г.	It snowed all day yesterday.
Вре́мя лети́т.	Time flies.
Но́вый америка́нский фи́льм идёт в кинотеа́тре «Росси́я».	A new American movie is playing at the movie theater "Russia."

C. Main contexts for using multidirectional verbs

In the previous examples, the unidirectional verb denotes a *one-way motion*. Contexts calling for an action that has *no direction* or takes place in *several directions* (including repeated motion along the same line) require the use of multidirectional verbs. The following list describes the most common contexts in which multidirectional verbs are used.

1. Motion in an indefinite, unspecified, random direction

> Ли́нда и Са́ша ча́сто хо́дят по у́лицам и переу́лкам Арба́та.
> Linda and Sasha often walk around the streets and side streets of the Arbat.

The multidirectional form is used to express random motion, i.e. motion proceeding in several or many directions. In this case, the verb is followed by the preposition **по** + the dative case to indicate "around" or "about" a given place.

Ли́нда хо́дит по го́роду и но́сит с собо́й пла́н го́рода.	Linda walks around the city and carries a city map with her.
Вчера́ мы́ ве́сь де́нь е́здили по го́роду.	Yesterday we drove around the city the whole day.
За́втра мы́ бу́дем ходи́ть по це́нтру Вашингто́на.	Tomorrow we are going to walk around downtown Washington.

2. Repeated or habitual motion

> Я всегда хожу за хлебом в магазин рядом с домом.
> I always go to the store next door to buy bread.

A repeated movement is not conceived of as proceeding in one direction, even though the goal of every individual repetition is stated. The overriding factor for Russian speakers is the *necessity to return to the starting point* in order to repeat the movement. This focus two directions rules out the unidirectional verb. Study the following examples.

Каждый день он ездит на работу на автобусе.
He rides to work every day by bus. *(He has to return home before he can go to work again.)*

Автобусы ездят в аэропорт и возят пассажиров.
The buses run to the airport and carry passengers.

Я часто хожу к своим друзьям.
I often go visit my friends.

Мы часто будем ходить к вам.
We'll come visit you often.

Борис очень любит кино. Он часто ходит в кинотеатр.
Boris really loves the movies. He goes to the movies a lot.

3. Generic description of motion

> Борис лю́бит ходи́ть пешко́м.
>
> Boris loves walking.

> Моя́ ба́бушка бои́тся лета́ть на самолёте.
>
> My grandmother is afraid of flying.

> Ребёнку то́лько го́д, но о́н уже́ хо́дит.
>
> The baby is only a year old, but he's already walking.

There are contexts that present motion as a characteristic feature of a person or object, as occurring habitually, or to indicate a person's ability or inability to perform an action. These meanings naturally exclude unidirectionality. As you can see in the following examples, multidirectional verbs indicating this kind of motion are often used with verbs such as **люби́ть, уме́ть,** and **боя́ться.**

Я не люблю́ бе́гать.	I don't like running.
Оле́г не уме́ет пла́вать.	Oleg doesn't know how to swim.
Я бою́сь е́здить с Серёжей.	I'm afraid to ride with Seryozha.
Он сли́шком бы́стро е́здит.	He drives too fast.

4. Round trips in the past tense

> Вчера́ Ли́нда и Са́ша ходи́ли в ци́рк. Они́ бы́ли в ци́рке.
>
> Yesterday Linda and Sasha went to the circus. They were at the circus.
>
> Вчера́ Ли́нда и Саша́ е́здили к Бори́су. Они́ бы́ли у Бори́са.
>
> Yesterday Linda and Sasha went over to Boris's. They were at Boris's.

When the subject makes a round trip in the past, this movement is viewed as multidirectional. The verbs **ходи́ть** and **е́здить** are used to convey a round trip *in the past tense only*[1].

In the examples below, note how the first sentence of each pair is synonymous with a similar sentence with the past tense of **бы́ть.**

— Где́ ты́ была́ вчера́?	"Where were you yesterday?"
— Я ходи́ла к врачу́.	"I went to the doctor's."
— Что́ вы́ де́лали в суббо́ту?	"What were you doing on Saturday?"
— Я е́здил к свои́м роди́телям.	"I went over to my parents'."

4. Carrying and transporting: transitive verbs of motion

There are three main pairs of transitive verbs of motion in Russian:

	Unidirectional Verb	*Multidirectional Verb*	*Definition*
Transitive	нести́	носи́ть	carry (while walking)
	везти́	вози́ть	carry (by vehicle)
	вести́	води́ть	lead

All of these verbs can take a direct object, and are used in the same contexts as their intransitive counterparts, as reflected in the following examples.

Unidirectional verbs:

Мно́гие иду́т к гардеро́бу и несу́т в рука́х пальто́.
Lots of people are walking toward the coat room and carrying their coats in their hands.

---

[1] The perfective verbs **сходи́ть** and **съе́здить** provide the only means of expressing a single round-trip in the future. See *Unit 7* and *Unit 10* for an explanation of these verbs.

Маши́ны е́дут к ци́рку, они́ везу́т зри́телей.
The cars are driving up to the circus, they are all carrying viewers (spectators).

Во́т идёт пожила́я же́нщина, ведёт за́ руку ма́льчика.
There goes an elderly woman, she is leading a small boy by the hand.
Multidirectional verbs:

Ли́нда хо́дит по го́роду и но́сит с собо́й пла́н го́рода.
Linda walks around the city and carries a map of the city with her.

Авто́бусы е́здят в аэропо́рт и во́зят пассажи́ров.
The buses go to the airport and take (transport) passengers.

5. Prefixed verbs of motion

A. The prefix по-: review

When the prefix **по-** is added to the unidirectional stem, the result is a perfective verb[1]. Verbs that have an irregular conjugation are listed in boldface.

Imperfective, Unidirectional Verb	Perfective Verb
идти́	**пойти́**
е́хать	**пое́хать**
лете́ть	полете́ть
бежа́ть	**побежа́ть**
плы́ть	поплы́ть
нести́	понести́
вести́	повести́
везти́	повезти́

---

[1] The prefix **по-** may also be added to multidirectional verbs of motion rendering a perfective that indicates that the action is limited *in time*. This temporal prefixation is analyzed in *Unit 10*. For now, only the addition of the prefix **по-** to unidirectional verbs is analyzed and practiced.

A perfective form with the prefix **по-** focuses specifically on the *beginning of or change in the action*, without specifying what happens next: "to *set out* walking (riding, flying, etc.)" The typical contexts for the perfective follow.

1. Embarking on a single action in the future

> Саша предложи́л мне́ пойти́ с ни́м в ци́рк.
>
> Сего́дня ве́чером мы́ пойдём в ци́рк.
>
> Sasha invited me to the circus. Tonight we're going to the circus.

The **по-** forms can indicate that someone is going or intends to go somewhere in the future.

В воскресе́нье я́ хочу́ пойти́ в теа́тр.	On Sunday I'm going to the theater.
За́втра мы́ пое́дем к ба́бушке.	Tomorrow we're going over to grandma's.
Ле́том они́ пое́дут в Москву́, а мы́ пое́дем в Ло́ндон.	This summer they're going to Moscow, and we're going to London.

The present tense of the unprefixed unidirectional verb can also be used to indicate an intended trip in the future, just as the present tense is used in English to signal a future action. The use of present tense forms to express future is restricted to statements about which the speaker is *more or less certain*, and also to statements which include modifiers of time showing that the action will be taking place *in the near future* (e.g., **за́втра, послеза́втра, через ча́с**).

Compare:

За́втра я́ пое́ду на экску́рсию.	Tomorrow I will go on an excursion.
За́втра я́ е́ду на экску́рсию.	Tomorrow I am going on an excursion.

If the action will not take place in the near future, the most likely choice is a perfective verb.

Этим ле́том мы́ пое́дем в Калифо́рнию.	This summer we're going to California.
В сле́дующем году́, я́ пое́ду в Росси́ю учи́ться.	Next year I'm going to Russia to study.

2. Embarking on a single action in the past

Past tense **по-** forms indicate that the subject has already set out, but gives no indication of whether or not s/he arrived at the destination or returned to the starting point.

— Где́ Ли́нда? — Её зде́сь не́т. Она́ пошла́ в магази́н.	"Where is Linda?" "She's not here. She went to the store."
— Са́ша до́ма? — Не́т, о́н пошёл в университе́т.	"Is Sasha home?" "No, he went to the university."
— Скажи́те пожа́луйста, Серге́й Ива́нович до́ма? — Не́т, о́н уже́ пое́хал на рабо́ту.	"Could you tell me, is Sergey Ivanovich home?" "No, he already went to work."
— Где́ все́ студе́нты? — Они́ пошли́ в кино́.	"Where are all of your students?" "They went to the movies."

Questions with past tense **по-** forms are used when the speaker is interested in whether or not someone has left already. Compare the following examples.

Ли́нда пошла́ в магази́н?	Has Linda left for the store yet?

Ли́нда ходи́ла в магази́н?	Has Linda gone to the store? (Has she been there?)

3. Shift or change in motion

> Прохо́жий отве́тил и пошёл, а точне́е побежа́л да́льше,
> наве́рное о́чень спеши́л.
> The passerby answered and set off, or rather ran off; he was
> probably in a hurry.

The prefix **по-** can also signal a change in motion. It emphasizes the beginning of a new direction or mode of action (such as speed).

Маши́на е́хала бы́стро, а перед шко́лой пое́хала ме́дленнее.	The car drove quickly, but began slowing down in front of the school.
Де́ти уви́дели ма́му и побежа́ли к ней.	The children saw their mother and took off running towards her.

4. Invitation

The **по-** forms are used in the first person future plural to express an invitation or exhortation.

Пойдём в кино́!	Let's go to the movies!
Пое́дем за́втра на вы́ставку!	Let's go to the exhibit tomorrow!

A stronger degree of persuasion is expressed by unprefixed unidirectional verbs in the same construction.

Идём в кино́!	Let's go to the movies! *(Let's be off already, let's definitely go!)*
Едем на вы́ставку!	Let's go to the exhibit! *(Let's be off already, let's definitely go!)*

B. Prefixes indicating direction

As you remember, prefixes for verbs of motion usually specify the *direction* (e.g., to, from, etc.) of an action. When a prefix is added to the basic verb pair, a new aspectual pair is formed. When a *multidirectional* stem is prefixed, it remains *imperfective*; when a *unidirectional* stem is prefixed, it becomes *perfective*.

Study the following examples of prefixed verbs of motion. Some of them may be familiar to you, while others are being introduced for the first time. Note that while all the verbs of motion—intransitive and transitive—can be prefixed, only the verbs formed by prefixing the basic intransitive pairs **éхать/éздить** and **идти́/ходи́ть** are actually practiced in *Unit 2*[1].

Imperfective	*Perfective*	*Definition*
приходи́ть	**прийти́**	come, arrive (on foot)
приезжа́ть	**прие́хать**	come, arrive (by vehicle)
уходи́ть	**уйти́-**	leave, depart (by foot)
уезжа́ть	**уе́хать**	leave, depart (by vehicle)
входи́ть	**войти́**	go in, enter (by foot)
въезжа́ть	**въе́хать**	go in, enter (by vehicle)
выходи́ть	**вы́йти**	go out, exit (by foot)
выезжа́ть	**вы́ехать**	go out, exit (by vehicle)
заходи́ть	**зайти́**	to drop by (by foot)
заезжа́ть	**зае́хать**	to drop by (by vehicle)

---

[1] See *Appendix XIII* for details on prefixation of other verb pairs.

cont.

Imperfective	Perfective	Definition
подходи́ть	**подойти́**	approach (on foot)
подъезжа́ть	**подъе́хать**	approach (by vehicle)
отходи́ть	**отойти́**	go away from (on foot)
отъезжа́ть	**отъе́хать**	go away from (by vehicle)

Note the following changes that occur with prefixation:

- when a prefix is added to the imperfective verbs **идти́, е́здить,** their forms change: **прийти́, приезжа́ть**;
- a hard sign "ъ" is inserted when the prefixes **в-, от-,** and **под-** (i.e., all those ending in consonants) are added to **е́здить** and **е́хать**;
- an "**о**" is inserted after the prefixes **в-, от-,** and **под-** (i.e., all those ending in consonants) before **-йти**.

Study the following examples of usage. Remember that the new aspectual pairs no longer indicate multi- or uni-directional motion. They conform to the general rules governing the choice of the imperfective or perfective aspect[1].

1. Arrival and departure: the prefixes **при-** and **у-**

> На ме́сто встре́чи я́ пришла́ во́время.
>
> I arrived at the meeting place on time.

> На спекта́кль мы́ опозда́ли и ушли́.
>
> We were late for the show and left.

The prefix **при-** adds the meaning of "arrival" to the basic meaning of the verb. It answers the question **«Куда́?»** and is used with the prepositions **в/на** + accusative and **к** + dative (for people).

---

[1] The use of an imperfective prefixed verb of motion to indicate "annulled action" is treated in *Unit 4, #4.*

Наташа придёт ко мне́ сего́дня ве́чером. Она́ ча́сто прихо́дит ко мне́.
Natasha will come over to my place tonight. She often comes over (visits
me).

Оле́г обы́чно приезжа́ет на рабо́ту в де́сять часо́в, но за́втра он
прие́дет в ча́с.
Oleg usually arrives at work at ten o'clock, but tomorrow he'll arrive at one.

The prefix **у-** is the opposite of **при-** and indicates "departure." It answers the question
«**Отку́да?**» and is accordingly used with the prepositions **из/с** + genitive and **от** +
genitive (for people).

Вчера́ у на́с бы́ли го́сти, и они́ ушли́ (от на́с) о́чень по́здно, бы́ло по́сле
двена́дцати.
We had guests over last night, and they left (from our place) really late, it
was after twelve.

Обы́чно я́ ухожу́ из до́ма на рабо́ту в во́семь часо́в, но сего́дня я ушёл
(ушла́) ра́ньше.
Usually I leave for work at eight o'clock, but today I left earlier.

Мы́ уезжа́ем в Росси́ю в пя́тницу.
We are leaving for Russia on Friday.

2. Entrance and exit: the prefixes **в-** and **вы-**

Я вошла́ в ко́мнату.
I entered the room.

Я вы́шла из ко́мнаты.
I exited (left) the room.

The prefix **в-** is used to indicate entrance into an enclosed space. It is most often used with the preposition **в** + accusative.

Она́ всегда́ вхо́дит в ко́мнату без сту́ка.
She always enters the room without knocking.

Нельзя́ входи́ть в за́л по́сле тре́тьего звонка́.
It is forbidden to enter the theater (hall) after the third bell.

Профе́ссор вошёл в аудито́рию и на́чал уро́к.
The professor entered the classroom and began the class.

The opposite of **в-** is **вы-**, indicating exit from an enclosed space. It is used with the prepositions **из/с** + genitive.

Ко́нчился фи́льм и зри́тели на́чали выходи́ть из зри́тельного за́ла.
The film ended and the viewers began to leave (exit from) the theater (viewing hall).

Ли́нда вы́шла из метро́ на ста́нции «Цветно́й бульва́р».
Linda exited the metro at the station "Tsvetnoy Boulevard."

The verb **выходи́ть/вы́йти** is also used colloquially to mean "to step out (briefly)."

(по телефо́ну)
— Попроси́те, пожа́луйста, к телефо́ну Серге́я Ива́новича.
— Он то́лько что вы́шел. Перезвони́те через де́сять мину́т.
"May I please speak to Sergei Ivanovich?"
"He just stepped out. Call back in ten minutes."

This use of **выходи́ть/вы́йти** always implies that the person is expected to return. If that is not the case and the person has actually left, then **уходи́ть/уйти́** is used.

3. Approach and movement (back) away from: the prefixes **под-** and **от-**

> К ци́рку подъезжа́ют маши́ны.
>
> Cars are pulling up to the circus.

> От ци́рка отъезжа́ют маши́ны.
>
> Cars are pulling away from the circus.

The prefix **под-** indicates approach or movement toward an object or thing. It is used with the preposition **к** + dative for both objects and people.

Он подошёл к окну́ и посмотре́л на у́лицу.
He walked up to the window and looked outside.

Такси́ подъе́хало к до́му и мы́ вы́шли.
The taxi pulled up to the building and we got out.

По́езд уже́ подхо́дит к платфо́рме.
The train is already approaching the platform.

Подходи́ть/подойти́ is the verb used in Russian to mean "walk up to someone/something."

Ната́ша подошла́ к профе́ссору и спроси́ла, когда́ у на́с бу́дет экза́мен.
Natasha walked up to the professor and asked when we would have an exam.

The opposite of **под-** is **от-** which indicates movement away from. It is used with the preposition **от** + genitive.

Поезд ужé отхóдит от платфóрмы.
The train is already leaving (moving away from) the platform.

Студéнт написáл задáние на доскé и отошёл (от доскú).
The student wrote the problem on the board and stepped back (from the board).

4. Movement past something: the prefix **про-**

> Мúмо меня́ пробегáют зрúтели.
> Viewers are running past me.

The prefix **про-**, when prefixed to basic pairs of verbs of motion, means "to pass by." It can be followed by a direct object in the accusative case, or it can be used with the preposition **мúмо** + genitive.

Я видéла егó сегóдня, нó óн меня́ не вúдел и прошёл мúмо меня́.
I saw him today but he didn't see me and he just passed by me.

Пя́тый автóбус не останáвливается здéсь. Он проезжáет мúмо э́той останóвки.
Bus number five doesn't stop here. It passes by this stop.

— Гдé здéсь Вторáя у́лица?
— Мы́ её ужé прошлú (проéхали).
"Where is Second Street around here?"
"We already passed it."

Уро́к 3: Когда́? Во ско́лько? На ско́лько?

1. Expressing clock time in Russian

> Сего́дня у́тром Ли́нда вста́ла в во́семь часо́в.
>
> This morning Linda got up at eight o'clock.
>
> Ли́нда обы́чно ложи́тся спа́ть в оди́ннадцать часо́в ве́чера.
>
> Linda usually goes to bed at eight o'clock p.m.
>
> Ли́нда свобо́дна по́сле шести́ часо́в ве́чера.
>
> Linda is free after six o'clock p.m.
>
> Они́ занима́ются с девяти́ до ча́са и с трёх до шести́ часо́в.
>
> They have class from 9:00 to 1:00 and from 3:00 to 6:00.

A. Equational sentences

Recall that the answer to the question, "What time is it?" («Ско́лько сейча́с вре́мени?» or «Кото́рый час?») can be expressed using the official 24-hour clock or colloquially.

24-hour system of expressing time

The 24-hour clock is used in public contexts such as radio and television broadcasts, transportation schedules, concerts, and sporting events.

8.20	во́семь часо́в два́дцать мину́т	8:20	AM
10.30	де́сять часо́в три́дцать мину́т	10:30	AM
14.15	четы́рнадцать часо́в пятна́дцать мину́т	2:15	PM
17.45	семна́дцать часо́в со́рок пя́ть мину́т	5:45	PM

Colloquial expression of time

The colloquial way of telling time is more complex than the 24-hour system. One construction is required if the time falls *in the first half* of the hour, and another if the time falls *in the second half* of the hour.

Use the following formula for a time falling in the first half of the hour (:01-:30).

nominative of minutes (cardinal) + genitive of the hour in progress (ordinal)

Thus, "1:05" is understood as "five minutes (elapsed) of the second hour" **«Пять минут второго»**. (The first hour is from twelve to one, the second is from one to two, the third is from two to three, etc.) Remember that ordinal numerals are adjectives and decline accordingly. The use of the word "minute(s)" is optional.

Сколько сейчас времени?

> Сейчас три минуты первого. (12:03)
> Сейчас пять минут третьего. (2:05)
> Сейчас двадцать две минуты четвёртого. (3:22)
> Сейчас двадцать пять минут десятого. (9:25)

Use the following formula for a time falling in the second half of the hour (:31-:59).

без + genitive of minutes (cardinal[1]) + nominative of hour in progress (cardinal)

Thus, "1:55" is understood as "minus five minutes two:" **«Без пяти минут два»**. The use of the word "minute(s)" is optional.

Note that numerals ending in **-ь** are third-declension feminine nouns. In compound numbers, all the elements are declined.

---

[1] See *Appendix IV* for declensions of cardinal numerals.

Ско́лько сейча́с вре́мени?

Сейча́с без двадцати́ ча́с. (12:40)
Сейча́с без пяти́ (мину́т) два́. (1:55)
Сейча́с без двадцати́ пяти́ ше́сть. (5:35)
Сейча́с без девяти́ (мину́т) во́семь. (7:51)
Сейча́с без (одно́й) мину́ты оди́ннадцать. (10:59)

The third-declension feminine noun **че́тверть** is used to denote "a quarter."

Сейча́с че́тверть (пятна́дцать мину́т) шесто́го. (5:15)
Сейча́с без че́тверти (пятна́дцати мину́т) четы́ре. (3:45)

To express "half-past," use the noun **полови́на** + genitive (ordinal) of the hour in progress. The word **полови́на** is often shortened to **пол-** and attached to the number for the hour in progress.

Ско́лько сейча́с вре́мени?

Сейча́с полови́на пе́рвого (полпе́рвого). (12:30)
Сейча́с полови́на второ́го (полвторо́го). (1:30)
Сейча́с полови́на четвёртого (полчетвёртого). (3:30)
Сейча́с полови́на восьмо́го (полвосьмо́го). (7:30)

B. "Time when" according to the clock

To express the time an action occurred in hours and minutes, the preposition **в** + the accusative case is used.

Сего́дня у́тром Ли́нда вста́ла в во́семь часо́в.
Linda got up this morning at eight o'clock.

Дава́йте встре́тимся в три́ часа́.
Let's meet at three o'clock.

Ле́кция начина́ется в два́дцать мину́т тре́тьего.
The lecture starts at 3:20.

Before **без** the preposition **в** is omitted.

Я прие́ду к ва́м без двадцати́ ше́сть.
I will come to your place at twenty to six.

Дава́йте встре́тимся без че́тверти се́мь.
Let's meet at a quarter to seven.

The expression "at half past..." constitutes an exception to the accusative "time when" rule. This expression requires the *prepositional case*.

Ле́кция начина́ется в полови́не пе́рвого.
The lecture starts at twelve thirty.

Компью́терный це́нтр закрыва́ется в полови́не деся́того.
The computer center closes at nine thirty.

Just like nouns, numbers denoting time must be put into the appropriate case after prepositions[1]. The prepositions **по́сле, о́коло** and **с... до...**+ genitive case are commonly used with time expressions.

Ли́нда обы́чно ложи́тся спа́ть о́коло оди́ннадцати часо́в ве́чера.
Linda usually goes to bed around eleven o'clock in the evening.

---

[1] See *Appendix IV* for declensions of cardinal numerals.

Ли́нда свобо́дна по́сле шести́ часо́в ве́чера.
Linda is free after six o'clock p.m.

Они́ занима́ются с девяти́ до ча́са и с трёх до шести́ часо́в.
They have classes (they study) from nine until one and from three until six.

У на́с заня́тия ка́ждый де́нь с девяти́ часо́в.
We have classes every day from nine o'clock on (beginning at nine o'clock).

Я рабо́таю ка́ждый де́нь до восьми́ часо́в ве́чера.
I work every day until eight o'clock in the evening.

Note how a.m. and p.m. are conveyed in Russian: the time expression is followed by the genitive singular of the words for morning, day, evening, and night: **утра́, дня́, ве́чера,** and **но́чи.**

2. Time when: days, weeks, months and seasons

Ли́нда хо́дит в бассе́йн в понеде́льник и в сре́ду.
Linda goes to the pool on Monday and Wednesday.
Ли́нда прие́хала в Москву́ о́сенью, в сентябре́.
Linda came to Moscow in the fall, in September.
Интенси́вный ку́рс на́чался на про́шлой неде́ле.
The intensive course began last week.

Review the following constructions for expressing "time when" an action takes place.

в + accusative (for periods shorter than a week)
на + prepositional (for "week")
в + prepositional (for periods longer than a week)

A. "Time when" for days of the week[1]

"Time when" for days of the week requires the preposition **в** + the accusative case.

Ли́нда хо́дит в бассе́йн в понеде́льник и в сре́ду.
Linda goes to the swimming pool on Monday and Wednesday.

У на́с бы́ло собра́ние в пя́тницу.
We had a meeting on Friday.

Экза́мен бу́дет во вто́рник.
The exam will be on Tuesday.

Мы́ пойдём в кино́ в суббо́ту.
We'll go to the movies on Saturday.

B. "Time when" for weeks

The preposition **на** + the prepositional case is used with weeks.

— Они́ бу́дут в Нью-Йо́рке на э́той неде́ле?	"Will they be in New York this week?"
— Не́т, они́ бы́ли в Нью-Йо́рке на про́шлой неде́ле.	"No, they were in New York last week."

---

[1] To express that an action takes place regularly on a certain day, the preposition **по** + the dative plural can be used.

У на́с всегда́ собра́ния по понеде́льникам.
We always have meetings on Mondays.

У меня́ семина́р по эконо́мике по среда́м.
I have an economics seminar on Wednesdays.

У на́с контро́льные рабо́ты по пя́тницам.
We have quizzes on Fridays.

[— Нéт, они́ бýдут в Нью-Йóрке   ["No, they'll be in New York next
на слéдующей (бýдущей) недéле.]   week."]

C. Units of time larger than a week

В + the prepositional case is used with periods of time longer than a week: months, semesters, years, decades, centuries, and millennia. This construction is also used when there are no specified time limits; e.g., "in the future," "in the past."

Ли́нда приéхала в сентябрé.   Linda arrived in September.

Макси́м роди́лся в январé.   Maxim was born in January.

Мы́ поéдем в Москвý в áвгусте.   We will go to Moscow in August.

в э́том мéсяце   this month
в э́том (прóшлом) семéстре   during/in this (last) semeseter
в прóшлом вéке   during/in the last century
в бýдущем   in the future
в прóшлом   in the past
в настоя́щем   in the present

Recall that expressing "year when" requires **в** + the ordinal number for the year + **годý**. Remember that *only the last component of the year number* is ordinal.

Онá родилáсь в ты́сяча девятьсóт сéмьдесят пя́том годý.
She was born in 1975.

Он окóнчил университéт в ты́сяча девятьсóт девянóсто шестóм годý.
He finished the university (graduated) in 1996.

D. Seasons of the year and parts of the day

As you already know, the seasons of the year and parts of the day constitute a special incidence among Russian expressions of "time when." These special adverbs must be memorized.

зимо́й in the winter	у́тром in the morning
весно́й in the spring	днём in the afternoon
ле́том in the summer	ве́чером in the evening
о́сенью in the fall	но́чью at night

Review the Russian way of stating the following common time expressions.

Сего́дня у́тром...	This morning...
Вчера́ днём...	Yesterday afternoon...
За́втра ве́чером...	Tomorrow evening...

3. The prepositions на and че́рез in time expressions

> Ли́нда прие́хала в Москву́ на де́сять ме́сяцев.
>
> Linda has come to Moscow for ten months.
>
> Че́рез де́сять ме́сяцев она́ пое́дет домо́й.
>
> She is going home in ten months.

A. The intentional на: "for" (a certain period of time)

На + accusative is used to express a period of time beginning after the action of the principal verb is completed. This construction is frequently used with verbs of motion to denote that a person has arrived or departed *for a certain period of time.*

— На ско́лько Ли́нда прие́хала в Москву́?
— Ли́нда прие́хала в Москву́ на де́сять ме́сяцев.

"For how long has Linda come to Moscow?"
"Linda has come to Moscow for ten months."

Они поедут в Петербург на неделю.
They are going to Petersburg for a week.

Мои друзья приедут ко мне на пять дней.
My friends are coming to see me for five days.

Я могу приехать к тебе только на один час.
I can come to your place (I can come to see you) only for an hour.

B. Expressing "in (or after)" (a certain amount of time)

Через + accusative denotes the time *after which* an action will occur or occurred.

— Когда Линда поедет домой?
— Линда поедет домой через
десять месяцев.

"When will Linda go home?"
"Linda will go home in (after) ten
months."

Мои родители приедут через неделю.
My parents will arrive in a week.

У нас будет экзамен через три дня.
We will have an exam in three days.

4. The prepositions за... до... to express time elapsing before an action

За + accusative... **до** + genitive... is used to indicate the time before the beginning of an action.

Линда пришла в цирк за пятнадцать минут до начала спектакля.
Linda arrived at the circus 15 minutes before the beginning of the
performance.

Я узнáла об э́том за двá дня́ до начáла семéстра.
I found out about that two days before the beginning of the semester.

Он получи́л письмó за недéлю до отъéзда.
He received the letter one week before his departure.

5. Expressing duration

A. Expressing duration of an action: imperfective verb without a preposition + accusative of time period

Ли́нда дéлает домáшнее задáние двáдцать мину́т.
Linda spends twenty minutes doing her homework.

To express the duration of an action, Russian uses an accusative form *without a preposition.* Note that the equivalent English phrases may or may not contain the preposition "for."

Мы́ бы́ли в Москвé одну́ недéлю.
We were in Moscow (for) one week.

Бори́с жи́л в Вашингтóне оди́н гóд.
Boris lived in Washington (for) a year.

Я рабóтаю в университéте пя́ть лéт.
I have been working at the university (for) five years.
(*Note that* **пять** *is the accusative here, and that a present tense is used to indicate an action that began in the past and is continuing into the present.*)

Я писáл(а) доклáд недéлю.
I wrote (worked on) the report (for) a week.

Мы́ учи́ли но́вые слова́ ве́сь ве́чер.
We studied the new words all evening.

Она́ переводи́ла э́тот рома́н два́ го́да.
She worked on translating the novel (for) two years.
(Note that два́ *is the accusative here.)*

B. Expressing "time in which" an action is completed: perfective verb used with
за + accusative of time period

Ли́нда сде́лала дома́шнее зада́ние за два́дцать мину́т.
Linda finished (completed) her homework in twenty minutes.

The time period required for the action of a perfective verb to be completed is conveyed by
the preposition за + accusative case. The equivalent meaning is generally rendered in
English by phrases with the preposition "in" (or "within").

Contrast this time expression with the durational accusative. За + accusative answers the
question, "How long did (will) it take to complete this action?" The durational accusative
answers the question, "How long did this action go on? (How long has it been going on?
How long will it go on?") without making any statement about completion.

Study the following examples.

Я написа́ла докла́д за неде́лю.
I wrote (and finished) the report in a week.

Мы́ вы́учили но́вые слова́ за ве́чер.
We learned all the new words in an evening.

Она́ перевела́ э́тот рома́н за два́ го́да.
She completed the translation in two years. *(Note that* два́ *is the accusative
here.)*

6. Нéкогда

Learn the Russian equivalent for the following expression.

> (I) have no time for...
>
> (Мне) нéкогда...

The logical subject is in the dative case; past is marked by **бы́ло** and the future is formed by using **бу́дет**. The infinitive is always imperfective.

> Мнé сегóдня нéкогда смотрéть телеви́зор. У меня́ за́втра экза́мен.
> I have no time to watch television today. I have an exam tomorrow.
>
> На э́той недéле на́м нéкогда бу́деть ходи́ть в кинó. Мы пи́шем курсову́ю рабóту.
> We don't have the time to go to the movies this week. We are writing our semester papers.
>
> Ему́ нéкогда бы́ло с на́ми разгова́ривать вчера́. Он бы́л óчень за́нят.
> He had no time to talk to us yesterday. He was very busy.

7. Simultaneous vs. sequential actions and aspect

A. Simultaneous actions

> Когда́ я́ э́то дéлала, я́ вспомина́ла сóн.
> While I was doing that, I remembered the dream.

Two imperfective verbs within the same sentence can signal that their actions are occurring simultaneously. Often simultaneity is signaled by such conjunctions as **пока́; и; в тó врéмя, ка́к;** and **когда́.**

Вчера́ я сиде́ла до́ма ве́сь ве́чер и писа́ла курсову́ю рабо́ту.
I sat (stayed) home all night last night and worked on my term paper.

Мы́ сиде́ли и разгова́ривали три́ часа́.
We sat and talked for three hours.

Ба́бушка пила́ чай и смотре́ла телеви́зор.
Grandmother drank tea and watched television.

В то вре́мя, ка́к Ли́нда и Са́ша е́хали в университе́т, они́ разгова́ривали и по-англи́йски, и по-ру́сски.
While Linda and Sasha were on their way to the university, they conversed in both English and Russian.

B. Sequential actions

Two or more single actions occuring sequentially are expressed using perfective verbs, and the meaning conveyed is that the first action is completed before the second has even begun, the second action is completed before the third, and so on. Remember that the perfective is only possible in the past or the future.

Ли́нда поста́вила буди́льник и легла́ спа́ть.
Linda set the alarm clock and went to bed.

Мы́ пообе́даем и пото́м пойдём в кино́.
We'll have lunch and then go to the movies.

However, a *series of actions that is repeated* in the past, present or future is expressed by the imperfective.

Ка́ждый де́нь я прихожу́ домо́й из университе́та, у́жинаю, смотрю́ но́вости по телеви́зору, де́лаю дома́шнее зада́ние и ложу́сь спа́ть.
Every day I get home from the university, have dinner, watch the news on TV, do my homework and go to bed.

8. Imperfective or perfective infinitive after certain verbs

A. Verbs followed by imperfective infinitives

The following verbs require that the accompanying infinitive be *imperfective*.

начина́ть/нача́ть	begin
конча́ть/ко́нчить	end
продолжа́ть/продо́лжить	continue
ста́ть	begin
перестава́ть/переста́ть	end, stop
устава́ть/уста́ть	grow tired
привыка́ть/привы́кнуть	get accustomed to
отвыка́ть/отвы́кнуть	get out of the habit of
учи́ться/научи́ться	learn
нра́виться/понра́виться	like
надоеда́ть/надое́сть	be (sick and) tired of

Мы́ на́чали занима́ться ру́сским языко́м то́лько в э́том году́.
We started studying Russian only this year.

Са́ша вчера́ ко́нчил составля́ть програ́мму.
Sasha finished writing the computer program yesterday.

Сего́дня мы́ продолжа́ем учи́ть но́вые слова́.
Today we are continuing to study new words.

B. Verbs followed by perfective infinitives

The following perfective verbs refer to a total event and are, therefore, necessarily followed by a *perfective* infinitive, regardless of their tense and whether or not they are negated.

забы́ть	forget
успе́ть	manage, have enough time
уда́ться	succeed, manage

Мы́ успе́ем вы́пить ча́шку ко́фе.
We have time to have a cup of coffee.

Я не успе́ю позвони́ть домо́й сего́дня.
I won't manage (have time) to call home tonight.

Я успе́ла зайти́ в магази́н перед обе́дом.
I managed to get to the store before lunch.

Са́ша забы́л поздра́вить Серёжу с днём рожде́ния.
Sasha forgot to wish Seryozha a happy birthday.

9. Verbs with the particle -ся (-сь): reflexive meaning[1]

The addition of the particle -ся[2] to the end of a verb can signal a variety of meanings. In *Unit 3* there are -ся verbs that have a *true reflexive* meaning; i.e. when the subject performs an action upon him/herself. Note that the reflexive pronoun is often omitted in English, since the idea of reflexivity is inherent in the meaning of the verbs themselves.

умыва́ть/ (кого́, что́) умы́ть	to wash (someone, something)	умыва́ться/ умы́ться	to wash up ("wash oneself")
одева́ть/ (кого́) оде́ть	to dress (someone)	одева́ться/ оде́ться	to get dressed ("dress oneself")
причёсывать/ (кого́) причеса́ть	to comb (someone's) hair	причёсываться/ причеса́ться	to comb or brush one's hair

[1] For other kinds of reflexive verbs with the particle -ся, see *Unit 5* and *Unit 9*.

[2] Recall that the particle -ся occurs after a final *consonant*, while -сь occurs after a final *vowel*.

Ма́ленькая де́вочка сама́ одева́ется, умыва́ется, причёсыватеся.
The little girl gets dressed, washes up, and brushes her hair all by herself.

Ли́нда бы́стро одева́лась.	Linda got dressed quickly.
Ли́нда одева́ла мла́дшую сестру́.	Linda dressed her little sister.

Ма́льчик са́м умыва́ется.	The little boy washes up all by himself.
Оте́ц умыва́л сы́на.	The father washed the little boy.

Ма́ма причёсывается.	Mom is brushing her hair.
Ма́ма причеса́ла де́вочку.	The mother brushed the little girl's hair.

10. The conjunctions по́сле того́, как; до того́, как; and перед те́м, как

You have seen the prepositions **до** + genitive, **перед** + instrumental and **по́сле** + genitive followed by nouns in the required case. When a verb clause follows the preposition, however, the basic conjunction is **то́, как** with **то́** in the required case, rendering the following conjunctions. Note that an infinitive often follows **как** when the subjects of the two clauses are the same. (These conjunctions are used in *Unit 3* and should be memorized.)

до того́, как: before

До того́, как написа́ть курсову́ю рабо́ту, Са́ша прочита́л мно́го кни́г по свое́й специа́льности.
Before writing his term paper, Sasha read a lot of books in his field.

перед те́м, как: just before

Перед те́м, как ле́чь спа́ть, Ли́нда поста́вила буди́льник на се́мь часо́в.
Just before going to sleep, Linda set the alarm clock for seven o'clock.

после того́, как: after

> Мы́ пойдём гуля́ть по́сле того́, как зако́нчим дома́шнее зада́ние.
> We'll go out after we finish our homework.

11. Common short-form adjectives[1]

> По́сле обе́да я́ всегда́ свобо́дна.
> I am always free after lunch.
> До дву́х часо́в мы́ бы́ли за́няты.
> We were busy until two o'clock.
> Через пя́ть мину́т о́н бу́дет гото́в.
> He will be ready in five minutes.

The following frequently-used short-form adjectives appear in *Unit 3*.

свобо́ден (свобо́дна, свобо́дны)	to be free, to be available
за́нят (за́нята, за́няты)	to be busy
гото́в (гото́ва, гото́вы)	to be ready

These short-form adjectives are always used *predicatively*, and therefore only occur in the nominative case. Only long-form adjectives can be used attributively[2]. Short-form adjectives are highly bound to a particular context and express *temporary* or *relational* qualities, whereas long-form adjectives express permanent features. Compare the meanings of the adjectives in the following examples.

---

[1] See *Unit 7, /8* and *Appendix X* for a detailed analysis of short-form adjectives.

[2] In other words, only a long-form adjective can be adjacent to the noun it modifies with no link-verb in between (e.g., "the <u>busy</u> student" as opposed to "the student *is* busy").

Short-form	Long-form
Мы бу́дем гото́вы через два́дцать мину́т. We'll be ready in twenty minutes. Ми́ша не́ был гото́в к экза́мену. Misha was not ready for the exam.	В э́том магази́не мо́жно купи́ть гото́вые блю́да. You can buy prepared foods in this store.
Са́ша свобо́ден то́лько по́сле пяти́ (часо́в). Sasha is free only after five (o'clock). Они́ бы́ли свобо́дны вчера́ до оди́ннадцати (часо́в). They were free yesterday until eleven (o'clock).	Всё своё свобо́дное вре́мя о́н прово́дит в компью́терном це́нтре. He spends all of his free time in the computer center. Пре́сса в Аме́рике счита́ется свобо́дной. The press in America is considered to be free.
Мы́ бы́ли за́няты вчера́ ве́чером. We were busy last night. Ната́ша бу́дет за́нята в суббо́ту. Natasha will be busy on Saturday. Оле́г за́нят ка́ждый де́нь по́сле рабо́ты. Oleg is busy every day after work.	На́ш дире́ктор о́чень за́нятый челове́к. Our director is a very busy person.

12. The emphatic pronoun са́м

The emphatic pronoun **са́м** (oneself, itself) is used to emphasize the noun or pronoun it modifies. Note that it must agree in number, gender, and case with its head word[1].

---

[1] Note that **са́м** follows the stress pattern of the pronouns **о́н**, **она́**, **оно́**, and **они́**, except that the nominative/accusative inanimate plural forms are stressed on the root.

		Masc.	Neuter	Fem.	Plural
Nom.		сáм	самó	самá	сáми
Accus.	(inanimate)	сáм	самó	самý	сáми
	(animate)	самогó	самогó	——	самúх
Gen.		самогó	самогó	самóй	самúх
Prep.		самóм	самóм	самóй	самúх
Dat.		самомý	самомý	самóй	самúм
Instr.		самúм	самúм	самóй	самúми

Дéвочка самá одевáется.
The little girl dresses herself.

Мúша сáм э́то сдéлает.
Misha will do that himself.

Мы́ сáми приготóвим обéд.
We'll cook lunch ourselves.

Окнó самó откры́лось.
The window opened by itself.

Note that in English the emphatic pronoun usually occurs at the end of the sentence, but in Russian it commonly occurs immediately after the noun or pronoun it modifies.

Урóк 4: Кáк óн (онá) вы́глядит? В чём óн (онá)?

1. Describing personal appearance

> Лѝнда вообщѐ похóжа на мáму, но у неё тёмные глазá, кáк у пáпы.
> Linda in general looks like her mother, but she has dark eyes like her father.

> Рядом стоя́ла симпатѝчная дéвушка с длѝнными рыжими волосáми.
> A nice-looking young woman with long red hair was standing nearby.

Use the following constructions to describe personal appearance.

A. Expressing resemblance: похóж

Recall that **похóж (похóжа, похóжи) на** + the accusative case is used to express that someone resembles another person. **Похóж** is a short-form adjective[1] like **свобóден, зáнят,** and **готóв,** which you saw in *Unit 3*.

Брáт и сестрá похóжи.	The brother and sister look alike.
Сы́н похóж на отцá.	The son looks like the father.
— На когó похóж Сáша?	"Who does Sasha look like?"
— Сáша похóж на отцá.	"Sasha looks like his father."
— Лѝнда похóжа на мáму ѝли на пáпу?	"Who does Linda look like, her mother or father?"
— Онá вообщѐ похóжа на мáму.	"In general, she looks like her mother."

---

[1] See *Unit 7* for a full analysis of short-form adjectives.

B. Physical traits and features: У кого́ что́...; Кто́ с че́м...

Note the use of the following expressions to describe physical traits and features.

> **у + person being described (genitive) + physical attribute (nominative)**

> У ма́мы зелёные глаза́ и краси́вая улы́бка.
> Mother has green eyes and a beautiful smile.

> У сестры́ ры́жие во́лосы и чёрные глаза́.
> My sister has red hair and dark eyes.

> У моего́ бра́та дли́нные, све́тлые во́лосы.
> My brother has long, light-colored hair.

> У ма́льчика симпати́чное лицо́.
> The little boy has a cute face.

> **person being described + с + attribute (instrumental)**

> У окна́ стоя́л мужчи́на с кру́глым лицо́м, с тёмными волоса́ми, и с чёрными уса́ми.
> A man with a round face, dark hair and a black mustache was standing by the window.

> У маши́ны стоя́л стари́к с седо́й бородо́й.
> An old man with a gray beard was standing by the car.

> Де́вушка была́ с больши́ми голубы́ми глаза́ми, с ры́жими волоса́ми.
> The girl had large blue eyes and red hair.

C. Expressions for describing clothing

Ко мне́ заходи́л молодо́й челове́к, высо́кий, стро́йный брюне́т,
в се́ром сви́тере и в джи́нсах.

A young man, a tall, thin brunette in a grey sweater and jeans, dropped by to see me.

To describe what someone is wearing, use the following construction:

person being described + в + clothing (prepositional)

Ко мне́ заходи́л челове́к в се́ром сви́тере и в джи́нсах.
A man in a gray sweater and jeans stopped by to see me.

— Ты́ не зна́ешь кто́ э́та же́нщина в си́нем пла́тье?
— В си́нем пла́тье? Не́т, не зна́ю.
"Do you know who that woman in the blue dress is?"
"In the blue dress? No, I don't know."

— В чём ты́ пойдёшь на ве́чер?
— Я наве́рное пойду́ в моём люби́мом костю́ме.
"What are you going to wear to the party?"
"I'll probably wear my favorite suit."

Expressions with the verbs **ходи́ть** and **носи́ть** can be used to indicate that someone regularly wears a given article or kind of clothing.

носи́ть + accusative

Она́ всегда́ но́сит кроссо́вки.
She always wears sneakers.

Он всегда́ но́сит очки́.
He always wears glasses.

ходи́ть в + prepositional

> Студе́нты здесь всегда́ хо́дят в джи́нсах и ма́йках.
> The students here always wear jeans and tee-shirts.

Note also the way to describe patterns in Russian:

> в кле́тку = plaid
> в поло́ску = striped
> в горо́шек = polka-dot

руба́шка в кле́тку	plaid shirt
ю́бка в поло́ску	striped skirt
костю́м в горо́шек	polka-dotted suit

D. Compliments

To say that something looks good on someone, the following construction is used:

person (dative) + идёт (иду́т) + article/color that looks nice (nominative)

> Тебе́ э́то пла́тье о́чень идёт.
> That dress becomes you.

> Ива́ну э́тот костю́м о́чень идёт.
> That suit looks really good on Ivan.

> Ли́нде о́чень иду́т но́вые очки́.
> Linda's glasses look really nice on her.

> Ва́м о́чень идёт кра́сный цвет.
> The color red looks very good on you.

Note that the appropriate response to a compliment is, **«Спаси́бо за комплиме́нт».**

2. The verb нра́виться/понра́виться

> Мне́ нра́вится лило́вое пла́тье. Оно́ мне́ сра́зу понра́вилось.
>
> I like the violet dress. I liked it immediately.

Recall the construction **кому́ нра́виться/понра́виться что́**. Note how the perfective is used to indicate a first-time assessment or judgement of a particular item, event, or action.

Мне́ нра́вится чёрный цве́т.
I like the color black.

Мне́ сра́зу понра́вился тво́й но́вый костю́м. Вообще́ мне́ нра́вится зелёный цве́т.
I liked your new suit right away (i.e. it made a good first impression on me).
In general I like the color green. (*The suit is presumably green.*)

3. Не + imperfective infinitive

> Я реши́л не подходи́ть.
>
> I decided not to go up to him.

A **negated infinitive** normally occurs in the *imperfective* aspect, as, for example, after such verbs as **по/обеща́ть, по/проси́ть, реша́ть/реши́ть,** and **по/сове́товать,** to indicate that a particular action did not, will not or should not take place. Note that the negative particle **не** stands directly before the infininive.

Обы́чно Ли́нда и Са́ша занима́ются вме́сте ве́чером, но сего́дня они́ реши́ли не встреча́ться.
Usually Linda and Sasha study together, but today they decided not to meet.

Андре́й попроси́л роди́телей не приходи́ть за́втра.
Andrey asked his parents not to come tomorrow.

Та́ня посове́товала мне́ не покупа́ть э́тот костю́м.
Tanya advised me not to buy that suit.

Likewise, an imperfective infinitive is also the norm after expressions denoting the unsuitability or futility of an action, such as **не на́до, не ну́жно, не сто́ит** (it's not worth....)

— Мне́ на́до купи́ть но́вый уче́бник. "I need to buy the new textbook."
— А мне́ не на́до покупа́ть.   "I don't have to.
Я его́ уже́ купи́л.   I already bought it."

За́втра суббо́та. На́м не на́до встава́ть ра́но.
Tomorrow is Saturday. We don't have to get up early.

Не сто́ит покупа́ть э́тот слова́рь.
That dictionary isn't worth buying.

4. Aspect and annulled action

Ната́ша сказа́ла мне́, что ко мне́ заходи́л молодо́й челове́к
Natasha told me that a young man stopped by to see me.

Imperfective forms are obligatory to express an act that was *accomplished and then undone* (or when the *results* of an action are *annulled*). This refers primarily to verbs denoting clearly "reversible" actions: open/close, give/take, get up/lie down, turn on/turn off, arrive/depart, bring/take, put on/take off, and others. Remember that the perfective of these verbs unambiguously stipulates that the one-way action is completed and its result is *still in force*; the imperfective is obligatory when the result has been neutralized or undone.

Included in this group of "reversible" actions are the following verbs.

открыва́ть/откры́ть	to open
закрыва́ть/закры́ть	to close
бра́ть/взя́ть	to take

оставля́ть/оста́вить	to leave
включа́ть/включи́ть	to turn on
вы́ключать/вы́ключить	to turn off
отдава́ть/отда́ть	to give back, return
надева́ть/наде́ть	to put on

Also included are many of the prefixed verbs of motion, both transitive and intransitive.

приходи́ть/прийти́	to arrive (by foot)
приезжа́ть/прие́хать	to arrive (by vehicle)
уходи́ть/уйти́	to depart (by foot)
уезжа́ть/уе́хать	to depart (by vehicle)
приноси́ть/принести́	to bring (by foot)
привози́ть/привезти́	to bring/deliver (by vehicle)
уноси́ть/унести́	to carry away (by foot)
увози́ть/увезти́	to carry away (by vehicle)

Analyze how the choice of aspect is affected by whether the results of an action are still in effect.

— Отку́да у тебя́ э́тот га́лстук?
— Я взял у бра́та. Тебе́ нра́вится?
"Where did you get that tie from?"
"I borrowed (took) it from my brother. Do you like it?"

— Я тебе́ звони́л(а) у́тром, но́ тебя́ не́ было до́ма. Где́ ты́ был?
— Я уходи́л в магази́н.
"I called you this morning but you were not home. Where were you?"
"I went out to the store." (*But I am obviously home now.*)

Мои́ друзья́ приезжа́ли ко мне́ на про́шлой неде́ле.
My friends came to see me last week. (*But they have left already.*)

Мои́ друзья́ прие́хали ко мне́ на про́шлой неде́ле.
My friends arrived last week. (*And they are still here.*)

Са́ша заходи́л к Ли́нде.
Sasha dropped by to see Linda. (*He is no longer there.*)

Са́ша зашёл к Ли́нде.
Sasha dropped by to see Linda. (*And he is still there.*)

5. The emphatic pronoun са́м, сама́, са́ми

> Мне́ само́й ну́жно пойти́ в магази́н.
>
> I have to go to the store myself.

Review the emphatic pronoun **са́м, сама́, са́ми** (oneself), which appeared in *Unit 3*. In this unit it is used in the dative (**самому́, само́й, сами́м**) with **ну́жно**.

Э́тот те́кст сло́жный, но́ мне́ самому́ (само́й) на́до его́ переводи́ть.
This text is difficult, but I have to translate it myself.

Де́тям сами́м на́до убира́ть свои́ игру́шки.
The children have to pick up their toys themselves.

Remember that in English the emphatic pronoun is often placed at the end of the sentence, whereas in Russian it is also commonly placed right after the noun or pronoun it emphasizes.

6. The verbs спра́шивать/спроси́ть and проси́ть/попроси́ть

These verbs are often confused because they are both expressed in English by the same word: "ask." Note that **спра́шивать/спроси́ть** means to ask a question in the sense of *asking for information*, whereas **проси́ть/попроси́ть** always means to *make a request* for someone *to do something*. Note also that **спра́шивать/спроси́ть** is never used with the noun **вопро́с** as a direct object; instead, the construction **задава́ть/зада́ть вопро́с** is used.

Compare the following examples and their English equivalents.

Ко́ля спроси́л, когда́ у на́с бу́дет экза́мен.
Kolya asked when our exam will be.

Спроси́ у Ната́ши, когда́ открыва́ется магази́н.
Ask Natasha when the store opens.

Мо́й сосе́д по ко́мнате попроси́л меня́ познако́мить его́ с мое́й семьёй.
My roommate asked me to (requested that I) introduce him to my family.

Я попрошу́ Воло́дю зайти́ к на́м ве́чером.
I'll ask (request) Volodya to drop by this evening.

Я хочу́ зада́ть ва́м оди́н вопро́с.
I would like to ask you one question.

Уро́к 5: Где́ мо́жно купи́ть...?

> Та́м продаю́тся ёлочные игру́шки, сувени́ры,
> нового́дние коро́бки конфе́т, продаю́т и ёлки.
>
> Christmas decorations, souvenirs, and boxes of candy are
> sold for New Year's; they sell Christmas trees, too.

1. More verbs with the particle -ся

Study the following synonymous Russian constructions: a) intransitive verbs with the reflexive particle **-ся**; b) transitive verbs without the particle **-ся** in the third-person plural without an explicit subject (and a direct object in the accusative case).

a. Та́м продаю́тся ёлочные игру́шки и сувени́ры.
   Christmans decorations and souvenirs are sold there.

b. Та́м продаю́т ёлочные игру́шки и сувени́ры.
   They sell Christmas decorations and souvenirs there.

a. По́чта открыва́ется в де́вять часо́в.
   The post office opens (is opened) at nine o'clock.

b. По́чту открыва́ют в де́вять часо́в.
   They open the post office at nine o'clock.

a. В э́том кинотеа́тре пока́зываются ста́рые фи́льмы.
   Old films are shown in this movie theater.

b. В э́том кинотеа́тре пока́зывают ста́рые фи́льмы.
   They show old films in this movie theater.

The grammatical subjects (nominative case) in all of the *a.* examples—**ёлочные игру́шки и сувени́ры, же́нская оде́жда, по́чта, ста́рые фи́льмы**—are, in fact, not agents performing actions on objects, but rather are undergoing the action themselves. In such cases the reflexive particle **-ся** is obligatory in Russian.

Here are more examples of this kind of reflexive.

Ле́кция начала́сь в семь часо́в.
The lecture began (was begun) at seven o'clock.

Авто́бус останови́лся.
The bus stopped (was stopped).

Уче́бный год конча́ется в ма́е.
The academic year ends in May.

2. Simple comparative of adjectives and adverbs

> Я ду́мала, что ста́рые кни́ги деше́вле, чем но́вые.
> I thought that old books were cheaper than new ones.

The following is a review of the formation of the simple comparative of adjectives and adverbs. Remember that the simple comparative of adjectives is indeclinable and functions ONLY predicatively ("This book is more interesting," as opposed to, "I've never read a more interesting book.") Only the simple or "synthetic" comparative is covered in this unit.

A. Formation of the simple comparative

The comparative degree of adjectives and adverbs is formed by adding the suffix -ee or -e to the stem.

	Positive Degree	*Adverb*	*Comparative*
interesting	интере́сный	интере́сно	интере́снее
beautiful	краси́вый	краси́во	краси́вее
fresh	све́жий	свежо́	свеже́е
tasty	вку́сный	вку́сно	вкусне́е
cheery	весёлый	ве́село	веселе́е
quick	бы́стрый	бы́стро	быстре́е

cont.

	Positive Degree	Adverb	Comparative
slow	ме́дленный	ме́дленно	ме́дленнее
bright	све́тлый	светло́	светле́е
dark	тёмный	темно́	темне́е
difficult	тру́дный	тру́дно	трудне́е
important	ва́жный	ва́жно	важне́е

The suffix -e is added to stems ending in **к, г, х,** and monosyllabic stems ending in **ст.** These consonants undergo the expected mutation before the suffix **-e**.

$$к \Rightarrow ч \qquad х \Rightarrow ч$$
$$г \Rightarrow ж \qquad ст \Rightarrow щ$$

The stress invariably falls on the syllable immediately preceding the ending.

	Positive Degree	Adverb	Comparative
expensive	дорого́й	до́рого	доро́же
loud	гро́мкий	гро́мко	гро́мче
quiet	ти́хий	ти́хо	ти́ше
soft	мя́гкий	мя́гко	мя́гче
stern	стро́гий	стро́го	стро́же
simple	просто́й	про́сто	про́ще
clean	чи́стый	чи́сто	чи́ще

Sometimes the suffix **-e** causes unpredictable changes in the stem. These comparative forms must be memorized.

	Positive Degree	Adverb	Comparative
light, easy	лёгкий	легко́	ле́гче
long	до́лгий	до́лго	до́льше
thin	то́нкий	то́нко	то́ньше
deep	глубо́кий	глубоко́	глу́бже
far	далёкий	далеко́	да́льше

cont.

	Positive Degree	Adverb	Comparative
high, tall	высóкий	высокó	вы́ше
wide	ширóкий	широкó	ши́ре
low	ни́зкий	ни́зко	ни́же
rare	рéдкий	рéдко	рéже
narrow	у́зкий	у́зко	у́же
close, nearby	бли́зкий	бли́зко	бли́же
short	корóткий	кóротко	корóче
sweet	слáдкий	слáдко	слáще

The suffix -**e** is added to a few stems that do not end in **к, г, x,** or **ст**. Here are some of the most common ones.

	Positive Degree	Adverb	Comparative
young	молодóй	мóлодо	молóже
rich	богáтый	богáто	богáче
cheap	дешёвый	дёшево	дешéвле

The following common adjectives have unpredictable, irregular comparatives that must be memorized.

	Positive Degree	Adverb	Comparative
big	большóй	мнóго	бóльше
little	мáленький	мáло	мéньше
good	хорóший	хорошó	лу́чше
bad	плохóй	плóхо	ху́же

B. Usage of adjectival comparative constructions

There are two possible comparative constructions: the comparative can be followed by **чéм** plus a noun in the nominative, or by the genitive case of the noun *without* **чéм**. Note that **чéм** is always preceded by a comma.

Анна ста́рше, че́м бра́т.	Anna is older than her brother.
Анна ста́рше бра́та.	
Этот хле́б свеже́е, че́м то́т.	This bread is fresher than that bread.
Этот хле́б свеже́е того́ (хле́ба).	
Францу́зские духи́ доро́же, че́м америка́нские.	French perfume is more expensive than American (perfume).
Францу́зские духи́ доро́же америка́нских.	
Голла́ндский сы́р вкусне́е, че́м че́ддер.	Dutch cheese is better than chedder.
Голла́ндский сы́р вкусне́е че́ддера.	

C. Usage of adverbial comparative constructions

When **че́м** follows the comparative of an *adverb*, the noun after it must be in the appropriate case, with any necessary prepositions repeated.

То́ля ходи́л к Ива́ну ча́ще, че́м к Ми́ше.
Tolya visited Ivan more often than he visited Misha.

То́ля ходи́л к Ива́ну ча́ще, че́м Ми́ша.
Tolya visited Ivan more often than Misha (visited Ivan).

Ки́ра писа́ла на́м бо́льше, че́м свои́м роди́телям.
Kira wrote to us more than she wrote to her parents.

Серге́й рабо́тал бо́льше, че́м ты́.
Sergey worked more than you did.

Either construction (with or without **чéм** after the comparative adverb) is possible if the nouns or pronouns denoting the objects compared are *the subjects* of the sentence and, consequently, *are in the nominative case.*

Сáша говори́т по-англи́йски лу́чше, чéм Вáня.
Сáша говори́т по-англи́йски лу́чше Вáни.
Sasha speaks English better than Vanya.

However, when it is *not* the subjects that are being compared, only the **чéм** construction is possible.

Мы́ потрáтили бóльше дéнег на óтдых в э́том году́, чéм в прóшлом.
We spent more money on our vacation this year than last year.

Я ви́жу Олéга чáще, чéм Ивáна.
I see Oleg more often than Ivan (than I see Ivan).

Ли́нда разговáривает с Сáшей чáще, чéм с Натáшей.
Linda talks with Sasha more often than (she talks) with Natasha.

Натáша помогáла Свéте бóльше, чéм Лáре.
Natasha helped Sveta more than she helped Lara.

D. Comparisons of inferiority

To express a comparison of inferiority (e.g. "less tall" or "less interestingly"), use **мéнее** with the positive degree of the adjective (either long- or short-form) or with the adverb. This usage is more characteristic of bookish styles.

Эта кни́га мéнее интерéсная, чéм тá.
This book is less interesting than that one.

E. Expressions with comparatives

Listed here for your reference are some common expressions with comparatives.

1. **ка́к мо́жно + comparative**   **as... as possible**
   ка́к мо́жно лу́чше   as well as possible
   ка́к мо́жно скоре́е   as quickly as possible

2. **чём..., тём...**   **the... the...**
   чём быстре́е, тём лу́чше   the sooner the better

3. **тём . . .**   **all/so much the . . .**
   тём лу́чше   all the better
   тём ху́же   so much the worse

4. **гора́здо...**   **"much" (intensifier)**
   гора́здо лу́чше   much better
   гора́здо ху́же   much worse
   гора́здо бо́льше   much more
   гора́здо деше́вле   much cheaper

5. **по- (prefix added**   **"a little bit...."**
   to comparative)
   побо́льше   a little bit more/bigger
   поме́ньше   a little bit less/smaller
   подеше́вле   a little bit cheaper
   пора́ньше   a little bit earlier

3. Second-person imperative: review

> Этот набо́р о́чень дорого́й, не покупа́й его́.
> That set is very expensive, don't buy it.

A. Formation of the second-person imperative

Add **-и(те)** to the basic stem of the verb if the stress falls on the **-и-** of the imperative. The stress of the imperative form is always the same as the stress in the first-person singular form of the verb. Hence, if the **-ý/-ю́** of the first-person is stressed, the imperative is formed with **-й(те).**

Stem (stressed in 1st. per. sg.)		End-stressed imperative
говори́-	(говорю́)	говори́(те)
писа́ˣ-	(пишу́)	пиши́(те)
сказа́ˣ-	(скажу́)	скажи́(те)
заказа́ˣ-	(закажу́)	закажи́(те)
дари́ˣ-	(дарю́)	дари́(те)
плати́ˣ-	(плачу́)	плати́(те)
люби́ˣ-	(люблю́)	люби́(те)

Before the imperative ending, consonant alternation occurs if there is a consonant alternation before *all* vocalic endings (which means *throughout the non-past form of the verb*), as in **-а-, -ова-,** and **-о-** -stem verbs (**пиши́те, скажи́те**). If there is a consonant alternation *in the first person singular only,* then there is no alternation in the imperative form (**плати́те, люби́те**).

If the **-и-** of the imperative is not stressed[1], it is dropped and the preceding consonants, except for **й**, take on a soft sign.

Stem-stressed stem	Stem-stressed imperative
ве́ри-	ве́рь(те)
оста́ви-	оста́вь(те)
вста́н-	вста́нь(те)
оде́н-	оде́нь(те)
знако́ми-	знако́мься(тесь)
отве́ти-	отве́ть(те)

---

[1] Three important Russian verbs with post-root stress nevertheless drop the **-и-** and thus constitute exceptions. They are the **-жа-** verbs **боя́-ся** (imperative **бо́йся, бо́йтесь**) and **стоя́-** (imperative **сто́й сто́йте**), and the **-а-** verb **смея́-ся** (imperative **сме́йся, сме́йтесь**)

Nothing is added to form stem-stressed imperatives with stem-final **й**.

чита́й(те)	успе́й(те)	организу́й(те)
занима́йся (занима́йтесь)	дава́й(те)	про́буй(те)
выбира́й(те)	да́й(те)	сове́туй(те)
зака́зывай(те)	откро́й(те)	волну́й(ся) (волну́йтесь)
	умо́й(ся) [умо́йте(сь)]	

The **и** is never dropped after a double consonant, regardless of stress.

по́мни(те)

B. Aspect in the imperative

The choice of aspect in the imperative reflects the basic meanings and contexts for aspectual usage discussed in *Unit 3*. Requests for a repeated action are conveyed by the imperfective imperative, whereas requests for a specific, one-time action are generally expressed by the perfective imperative.

In the following examples, an imperfective imperative is used to give advice or instructions to do something regularly.

Покупа́йте проду́кты в э́том магази́не, здесь всё деше́вле.
Buy your groceries in this store, everything is cheaper here.

Помога́йте мла́дшему бра́ту де́лать дома́шнее зада́ние ка́ждый де́нь.
Help your younger brother do his homework every day.

Обяза́тельно гуля́йте ка́ждый ве́чер по́сле у́жина, э́то поле́зно для здоро́вья.
Definitely walk (take a walk) every evening after dinner, it's healthy.

Note how the perfective aspect is typically used for commands or requests to perform a single, complete action.

> Позвони́ ему́ и узна́й, ка́к о́н себя́ чу́вствует.
> Call him and find out how he is feeling.

> Подари́ е́й компа́ктный ди́ск на де́нь рожде́ния.
> Give her a CD for her birthday.

> Покажи́те, пожа́луйста, э́ту шля́пу.
> Please show me that hat.

> Купи́те мне́, пожа́луйста, сы́р и молоко́.
> Please buy me cheese and milk.

An imperfective imperative is used as a cue or reminder to perform an action, or a prompt for someone to proceed with an action that follows automatically from the situation. Two basic types of cue-situations may be distinguished.

Social conventions
Within social situations, a limited number of imperfectives functioning as "cues/reminders" are essentially formulaic.

A host will use the following imperative forms with guests.

> Входи́те.   Come/go in.
> Раздева́йтесь, пожа́луйста.   Please take off your coat.
> Сади́тесь, пожа́луйста.   Please sit down/have a seat.

A waiter/waitress will say to a customer:

> Зака́зывайте, пожа́луйста.   Your order, please.

Prompting

In each of the following examples, the preceding context sets the stage for the command to prompt the listener to **begin** a certain action.

> Вы́ прочита́ли пе́рвую главу́? Чита́йте втору́ю.
> Did you finish reading the first chapter? Read the second one.

> Вы́ написа́ли пе́рвое упражне́ние? Пиши́те сле́дующее.
> Have you finished writing the first exercise? Write the next one.

Sometimes this prompting of the beginning of the action is expressed by the use of an imperfective verb *after its perfective counterpart* to provide further *encouragement* (*exhortation* or *incitement*) to perform the action concerned.

> Расскажи́, что́ бы́ло пото́м. Почему́ ты́ молчи́шь? Расска́зывай!
> Tell me what happened next. Why aren't you saying anything? Go ahead, tell me (begin)!

> Запиши́те мо́й телефо́н. У ва́с е́сть ру́чка? Ну во́т, пиши́те....
> Write down my telephone number. Do you have a pen? OK, write it....

> Возьми́те мо́й уче́бник до за́втра. Он мне́ не ну́жен сего́дня. Бери́те, бери́те.
> Take my book until tomorrow. I don't need it today. Go ahead, take it, take it.

C. Aspect in the negative imperative

Unlike the positive commands discussed above, there is no aspectual choice to be made when making a request *not* to perform a given action. Here the *imperfective aspect* is the rule.

> Не расска́зывай ему́ об э́том.
> Don't tell him about that.

> Не покупа́й э́ту матрёшку, она́ сли́шком дорога́я.
> Don't buy that nesting doll, it is too expensive.

Не спра́шивайте меня́ об э́том, я́ ничего́ не зна́ю.
Don't ask me about that. I don't know anything.

There is one instance when a perfective verb may be used: to express a warning against an inadvertent action that will lead to negative (at the least undesirable, perhaps even dangerous) results. Such expressions are often accompanied by words of warning like **смотри́** and **осторо́жно.**

> *To a roommate who is on his/her way out:*
> Не забу́дь ключи́, меня́ не бу́дет до́ма ве́чером.
> Don't forget your keys, I won't be home this evening.

> *To a classmate about an important exam:*
> Смотри́, не опозда́й на экза́мен, о́н начина́ется ро́вно в де́сять часо́в.
> Don't be late for the exam, it begins exactly at ten o'clock.

> Осторо́жно, не наступи́ на стекло́, я́ разби́ла стака́н.
> Be careful, don't step on the glass, I broke a glass.

4. Aspect and the modal word нельзя́

> Но в дверя́х бы́ло та́к мно́го люде́й, что́ нельзя́ бы́ло войти́.
> But there were so many people at the doors that it was impossible to enter.

The modal word **нельзя́** deserves special comment because it has two possible meanings: "it is not possible," and "it is not allowed/it is forbidden." When **нельзя́** is followed by a *perfective* infinitive, it indicates *impossibility*. When it is a matter of *permission/prohibition*, **нельзя́** must be followed by an *imperfective* infinitive.

Contrast the following examples.

В ко́мнату нельзя́ войти́, у на́с не́т ключа́.   *It's physically impossible.*
We can't (it's impossible to) get into the room,
we don't have a key.

В ко́мнату нельзя́ входи́ть, та́м идёт репети́ция.
We can't go into the room, there's a rehearsal in progress.

It's unadvisable, "forbidden."

Во все́х зда́ниях университе́та нельзя́ кури́ть.
Smoking is forbidden in all buildings of the university.

It's forbidden.

Та́м нельзя́ оставля́ть маши́ну, та́м штрафу́ют.
It's illegal to park there, you'll get a ticket.

It's forbidden.

Отсю́да нельзя́ позвони́ть, телефо́н не рабо́тает.
It's impossible to call from here, the phone doesn't work.

It's physically impossible.

Note that in the past and future, **нельзя́** is used with the neuter singular form of **бы́ть**. Remember that this is an impersonal construction, and if the logical subject is expressed, it is in the dative case.

5. Review of double negation rule

Recall that negated verbs in Russian must be used with negated pronouns and adverbs, creating a double negative in Russian. Negated adverbs and pronouns are formed by adding the prefix **ни-**.

Pronouns

кто́	who	никто́	no one, nobody
что́	what	ничто́	nothing
како́й	which	никако́й	no kind (of), not any
че́й	whose	ниче́й	no one's

Adverbs

когда́	when	никогда́	never
где́	where	нигде́	nowhere
куда́	to where	никуда́	to nowhere
отку́да	from where	ниотку́да	not from anywhere

Review the following examples.

Никто́ не зна́ет, где́ Са́ша.	No one knows where Sasha is.
Я ничего́ не купи́ла.	I didn't buy anything.
Мы́ никуда́ не ходи́ли вчера́.	We didn't go anywhere yesterday.
Я ещё никому́ не звони́л.	I haven't called anyone yet.

Note that if a negative pronoun is the object of a preposition, the preposition is placed *between* **ни-** and the pronoun. The three elements are pronounced as a single phonetic unit.

Ни у кого́ не́ было де́нег.	No one had any money.
Ли́нда ни о ко́м ни забы́ла, когда́ она́ покупа́ла пода́рки.	Linda didn't forget anyone when she was buying presents.
Он ни с ке́м не говори́л об э́том.	He didn't talk to anyone about that.

Уро́к 6: Прия́тного аппети́та!

1. Verbs of position and positioning

> На полу́ лежи́т большо́й ковёр.
>
> A large carpet is on the floor.

> Он положи́л моде́ль на́ пол.
>
> He put the model on the floor.

There are four sets of positional verbs that are very frequently used in both the spoken and written language. The scheme below is intended to show the symmetries among forms and functions within this important group. The stative and causative verbs, as well as the assumptive verb **сади́ться/се́сть**, are the focus of this unit. The other two assumptive verbs, **ложи́ться/ле́чь** and **встава́ть/вста́ть**, appear in *Unit 3*.

Stative Verbs (All Intransitive) Где́?	Causative Verbs (All Transitive) Куда́?	Assumptive Verbs (All Intransitive)
"be in a certain position"	"put into a certain position"	"assume a certain position"
лежа́ть to be in a lying position	кла́сть/положи́ть to put into a lying position	ложи́ться/ле́чь to assume a lying positon, to lie down
сиде́ть to be in a sitting position	сажа́ть/ посади́ть to put into a sitting position (to seat)	сади́ться/се́сть to take a seat, to be seated
стоя́ть to be in a standing position	ста́вить/поста́вить to put into a standing position	встава́ть/вста́ть to assume a standing position, to stand up
висе́ть to be in a hanging position	ве́шать/пове́сить to hang up	*none*

Note the following features of these special verbs:

- Stative verbs have no perfective aspectual counterparts, since by definition they indicate a state or process.

- All the stative verbs are second conjugation verbs with stress on the ending.

- The perfective counterparts of the causative verbs are all prefixed with **по-** and belong to the second conjugation.

- The first two assumptive verbs are unusual for Russian: the imperfective forms end in **-ся**, the perfective forms do not.

- Note that the stative verbs are intransitive verbs seen to express *location*, and therefore are often followed by **в, на** + prepositional case (or **за** + instrumental). In contrast, the causative verbs are all transitive verbs seen as implying *motion in a certain direction*, and therefore are followed by **в, на, за** + accusative case.

- The assumptive verbs are intransitive.

Contrast the following examples.

Где стои́т, лежи́т, сиди́т, виси́т...?

Куда́ поста́вить, положи́ть, пове́сить, посади́ть...?

Ла́мпа стои́т на столе́.
The lamp is (standing) on the table.

Я ста́влю ла́мпу на сто́л.
I am placing the lamp on the table.

Газе́ты лежа́т на по́лке.
The newspapers are lying on the shelf.

Он всегда́ кладёт газе́ты на по́лку.
He always puts the newspapers on the shelf.

Карти́на висе́ла на стене́.
The painting was hanging on the wall.

Она́ пове́сила карти́ну на сте́ну.
She hung the painting on the wall.

Го́сти сидя́т за столо́м.
The guests are sitting at the table.

Хозя́йка посади́ла госте́й за сто́л.
The hostess seated the guests at the table.

2. Case usage and verbs after numbers

A. Review of cases after numerals

1. The numeral one

Оди́н (одна́, одно́, одни́) functions like a modifier, agreeing in gender, number and case with the noun it modifies.

У меня́ одна́ ви́лка.	I have one fork.
У нас то́лько оди́н хоро́ший нож.	We only have one good knife.
Одно́ пальто́ ещё виси́т у две́ри.	One coat is still hanging by the door.

There are instances when the numeral *one* can be plural: when it modifies a noun that occurs *only in the plural*.

одни́ брю́ки	one pair of pants
одни́ золоты́е часы́	one gold watch
одни́ но́жницы	one pair of scissors

The numeral one can also be used in the plural to mean "only."

У меня́ то́лько оди́н до́ллар.	I have only a dollar.
У меня́ одни́ хоро́шие джи́нсы.	I have only one (pair of) good jeans.

2. Other numerals

The numerals 2 (masc., neut. **два**; fem. **две**), 3, 4, and their compounds (e.g. 22, 23, 24; 32, 33, 34) function as noun-quantifiers and govern the *genitive singular*. The numerals 5 and above, including the numerals 12, 13, and 14, also function as noun-quantifiers and govern the *genitive plural*. Note that this applies only when the number quantifies either the subject or an inanimate direct object.

оди́н компью́тер	два́ компью́тера	пя́ть компью́теров
оди́н то́рт	два́ то́рта	пя́ть то́ртов
одна́ ло́жка	две́ ло́жки	пя́ть ло́жек
одна́ буты́лка	две́ буты́лки	пя́ть буты́лок
одно́ окно́	два́ окна́	пя́ть о́кон
одно́ яйцо́	два́ яйца́	пя́ть яи́ц

3. Adjectives and numerals

An adjective in the genitive plural can be used after all numbers except *one*; after *one*, the adjective agrees with the noun it modifies.

оди́н большо́й компью́тер	два́ больши́х компью́тера	пя́ть больши́х компью́теров
одна́ золота́я ло́жка	две́ золоты́х ло́жки	пя́ть золоты́х ло́жек
одно́ ма́ленькое окно́	два́ ма́леньких окна́	пя́ть ма́леньких о́кон

4. Numerals and verb agreement

When the subject of a sentence is a numeral greater than one, the accompanying verb can be in the third-person neuter singular or plural.

В холоди́льнике стои́т/стоя́т четы́ре буты́лки молока́.
There are four bottles of milk in the refrigerator.

На столе́ стои́т/стоя́т два́ компью́тера.
There are two computers on the table.

В на́шей гру́ппе у́чатся/у́чится два́дцать студе́нтов.
Twenty students study in our group.

Quantifiers such as **мно́го, ма́ло, не́сколько,** and **ско́лько** require the neuter singular form of the verb.

На полу́ лежа́ло мно́го игру́шек.
A lot of toys were lying on the floor.

На таре́лке бы́ло не́сколько пирого́в.
There were a few pies on the plate.

Ско́лько кни́г стои́т на по́лке?
How many books are on the shelf?

3. Instrumental case in definitions and descriptions

> Пироги́ с мя́сом, пироги́ с капу́стой, пироги́ с гриба́ми.
> Meat pies, cabbage pies, mushroom pies.

You are already familiar with the following uses of the instrumental case.

- to express instrument or agent of action (without a preposition)
- to mean "accompanied by," with," or "along with" (after the preposition **с**)
- in equational sentences in the past or future
- with certain verbs

In *Unit 6*, the preposition **с** + instrumental is used to define or describe an object. This usage is particularly common with food. Here are some examples.

бутербро́д с сы́ром	cheese sandwich
пироги́ с мя́сом	meat pies
омле́т с ветчино́й	ham omelet

ватру́шка с тво́рогом   cheese danish
ко́фе с молоко́м   coffee with milk

4. The indefinite particles -то and -нибудь

Пото́м Ири́на принесла́ ещё каки́е-то други́е горя́чие блю́да.
Then Irina brought in some other kinds of hot dishes.

Ли́нда, тебе́ что́-нибудь нали́ть?
Linda, can I pour you something?

Recall that the indefinite particles **-то** and **-нибудь** are added to the pronouns **како́й, кто́,** and **что́,** and the adverbs **когда́, где́,** and **куда́** to create indefinite pronouns and adverbs.

A. The particle -то

The particle **-то** imparts the meaning of "definite but unspecified." The person, thing, place, or time is definite, but for some reason the speaker chooses not to identify it, either because s/he doesn't know or chooses not to say.

В рука́х у него́ была́ кака́я-то игру́шка.
He was holding some sort of toy.

Он расска́зывал о чём-то интере́сном.
He was telling about something interesting.

Мы́ пи́ли что́-то о́чень вку́сное.
We drank something very tasty.

Э́то како́й-то о́чень вку́сный со́ус.
This is some sort of very good (tasty) sauce.

Пото́м бы́ли ещё каки́е-то други́е горя́чие блю́да.
Then there were some other hot dishes.

The word **что́-то** has a special meaning in addition to the one discussed above. It is used in conversational Russian to mean, "for some reason."

> Что́-то мне́ не нра́вится э́тот челове́к.
> For some reason I don't like that person.

> Что́-то я́ ника́к не пойму́, что́ здесь происхо́дит.
> For some reason I can't understand what is going on here.

B. The particle -нибудь

Pronouns with the particle **-нибудь** are typically encountered in questions and imperative sentences. In questions, these pronouns and adverbs indicate that the speaker is unaware of what (who) the agent, object, or place of action might be.

> Ли́нда, тебе́ что́-нибудь нали́ть?
> Linda, can I pour you something?

> Мне́ кто́-нибудь звони́л?
> Did anybody call me?

In requests, they indicate that the speaker has no preference or is undecided about what (who) the agent, object, or place of action is.

> Сади́сь куда́-нибудь.
> Sit down anyplace (you like).

> Да́й мне́, пожа́луйста, что́-нибудь пое́сть
> Please give me something to eat.

> Купи́, пожа́луйста, что́-нибудь сла́дкое.
> Please buy something sweet.

5. First-person imperative: "Let's...!"

> Давáйте пить винó.
>
> Let's drink wine.
>
> Давáйте выпьем за здорóвье Иры!
>
> Let's drink to Ira's health!

Recall that the first-person imperative is used to express "Let's...," whereby the speaker includes him/herself in a suggestion, invitation, or exhortation. Review the following rules for the formation of the first-person imperative.

For imperfective verbs:
Давáйте + infinitive

Давáйте обéдать.	Let's eat lunch.
Давáйте смотрéть вúдео.	Let's watch a video.
Давáйте слýшать мýзыку.	Let's listen to music.

For perfective verbs:
Давáйте + first-person plural (future perfective)

Давáйте кýпим шампáнское.	Let's buy champagne.
Давáйте выпьем за здорóвье Иры!	Let's drink (toast) to Ira's health!
Давáйте уберём со столá.	Let's clear the table.

6. Third-person imperative

> Пу́сть Бори́с пока́жет тебе́ кварти́ру.
>
> Let Boris show you the apartment.

The third-person imperative is expressed by inserting the word **пу́сть** (or colloquially, **пуска́й**) before the subject (person) performing the action. Note that **пу́сть** is equivalent to the English "let" or "have."

Пу́сть Бори́с пока́жет кварти́ру.
Let Boris show (you) the apartment.

Пу́сть Ли́нда ку́пит то́рт, а мы́ ку́пим цветы́.
Let Linda buy a cake, and we'll buy flowers.

Пу́сть Са́ша помо́жет на́м.
Have (let) Sasha help us.

7. Пора́

> На́м пора́ уходи́ть!
>
> It's time for us to leave!

Пора́ is used in impersonal constructions and when followed by an imperfective infinitive it means "It is time to begin a certain action." If the logical subject is specified, it is in the dative case.

Мне́ пора́ уходи́ть!
It's time for me to leave.

Пора́ сади́ться за сто́л!
It's time to sit down (at the table)!

Де́тям пора́ ложи́ться спа́ть.
It's time for the children to go to bed.

На́м пора́ накрыва́ть на сто́л, ско́ро прие́дут го́сти.
It's time for us to set the table, the guests will arrive soon.

The third-person neuter singular form of **бы́ть** is added to express past and future.

Мне́ пора́ бы́ло уходи́ть.
It was time for me to leave.

Ско́ро на́м пора́ бу́дет уходи́ть.
It will soon be time for us to leave.

На́м пора́ бы́ло собира́ть ве́щи.
It was time for us to gather/pack our things.

На́м ско́ро пора́ бу́дет собира́ть ве́щи.
It will soon be time for us to pack our things.

8. Expressing a plural subject

Вчера́ мы́ с Са́шей ходи́ли в го́сти к Ири́не и Бори́су.

Yesterday Sasha and I went to visit Irina and Boris.

Review this very common way of expressing a plural subject.

plural pronoun + **с** + person in the instrumental case

> мы́ с Са́шей = Sasha and I
> вы́ с Ирой = you and Ira
> они́ с Ната́шей = he (or she) and Natasha

Вчера́ мы́ с Са́шей ходи́ли в го́сти к Ири́не и Бори́су.
Yesterday Sasha and I visited Irina and Boris.

Мы́ с Та́ней купи́ли Ире цветы́.
Tanya and I bought Ira flowers.

Вы́ с Андре́ем уже́ ходи́ли в магази́н?
Have you and Andrey already been to the store?

If the logical subject is in a case *other than the nominative*, this is reflected in the plural pronoun part of the construction; the noun or pronoun following the preposition **с** does not change.

Ва́м с Ива́ном на́до купи́ть пода́рок Ли́нде.
You and Ivan have to buy a present for Linda.

На́м с ва́ми на́до пойти́ в магази́н.
You and I have to go to the store.

На́м с тобо́й на́до занима́ться. У на́с за́втра экза́мен.
You and I have to study. We have an exam tomorrow.

Ва́м с Серге́ем на́до поздра́вить Иру.
You and Sergei have to congratulate Ira.

9. Review of relative clauses: кото́рый

Clauses that qualify nouns are called *relative clauses*. Here is an example of a relative clause in English:

The book *that I read* was interesting.

In Russian, the relative pronoun **кото́рый** (equivalent to "which," "who," and "that") is used to introduce a relative clause. **Кото́рый** agrees in gender and number with its antecedent, but its case depends upon its function in the relative clause. Note that a comma *always precedes* **кото́рый**.

Я ходи́л(а) в теа́тр с дру́гом, кото́рый неда́вно прие́хал в Москву́.
I went to the theater with my friend who arrived in Moscow recently.

Я говорю́ об актёрах, кото́рые игра́ют в э́том спекта́кле.
I am talking about the actors who are in that show.

Note the placement and use of prepositions governing **кото́рый**.

Я бы́л(а́) на вы́ставке, о кото́рой вы́ мне́ расска́зывали.
I have been to the exhibit that (which) you told me about.

Это до́м-музе́й, в кото́ром жи́л и рабо́тал Достое́вский.
This is the residence-museum in which (where) Dostoevsky lived and worked.

Вчера́ мы́ ходи́ли в галере́ю, в кото́рой сейча́с идёт вы́ставка молоды́х
абстракциони́стов.
Yesterday we went to the gallery where there is an exhibit of young abstractionists.

Это на́ши бли́зкие друзья́, с кото́рыми мы́ отдыха́ли в про́шлом году́.
These are our close friends with whom we vacationed last year.

An active review of **кото́рый** is included in *Unit 7*. It is provided here for you to review
before you encounter verbal adjectives (participles) in the next section.

10. Verbal adjectives (participles) for reading

You will encounter verbal adjectives in the *Reading* days of *Units 6-10*. Though not
common at this stage of study in spoken Russian, verbal adjectives are common in the
written language, especially in literary, journalistic, academic, scientific and expository
prose. These grammatical forms are intended for *passive knowledge* only, for the purpose
of developing reading skills. You will be expected to recognize verbal adjectives and
identify them as passive or active, and as present or past[1]. You will *not* be expected to form
them, and work with them is restricted primarily to workbook exercises.

---

[1] There are no future participles.

A. Usage of long-form verbal adjectives (participles)

A participle in Russian is a part of speech which may take the place of both the relative pronoun and the verb of the relative clause it introduces. Participles are formed by adding a suffix to the basic stem of the verb. This form (together with its adjuncts, if any), like the relative clause that it replaces, still qualifies some noun in the sentence and so has adjectival endings.

Long-form verbal adjectives (participles) can be used to replace the relative pronoun **кото́рый** and the verb of the relative clause it introduces IF, and only if, the relative pronoun is in the nominative or accusative case.

There are two kinds of participles: active and passive. Relative clauses introduced by **кото́рый** in the nominative case can be replaced by phrases with *active* participles. Relative clauses introduced by **кото́рый** in the accusative case can be replaced by phrases with *passive* participles.

Participles are rarely encountered by themselves. They are generally used with various qualifiers and together with them make up participle constructions. Participles or participle constructions may either precede or follow the noun they qualify. In the latter case, they must be set off by commas.

Study the following examples, paying particular attention to the difference in the English translations.

1. **кото́рый** in the *nominative* case and a present-tense verb ➜ present *active* participle

   Ма́льчик, кото́рый чита́ет кни́гу, сиди́т за столо́м.
   The little boy who is reading the book is sitting at the desk.

   Ма́льчик, чита́ющий кни́гу, сиди́т за столо́м.
   The little boy reading the book is sitting at the desk.

2. **кото́рый** in the *nominative* case and a past-tense verb ➜ past *active* participle

   Ма́льчик, кото́рый чита́л кни́гу, оста́вил кни́гу на столе́.
   The boy who was reading the book left the book on the desk.

Мáльчик, читáвший кнúгу, остáвил кнúгу на столé.
The little boy, having read the book, left the book on the desk.

3. **котóрая** in the *accusative* case and a present-tense verb ➜ present *passive* participle

Кнúга, котóрую читáет мáльчик, óчень интерéсная.
The book that the boy is reading is very interesting.

Кнúга, читáемая мáльчиком, óчень интерéсная.
The book being read by the boy is very interesting.

4. **котóрая** in the *accusative* case and a past-tense verb ➜ past *passive* participle

Кнúга, котóрую прочитáл мáльчик, óчень интерéсная.
The book which the boy has read is very interesting.

Кнúга, прочúтанная мáльчиком, óчень интерéсная.
The book read by the boy is very interesting.

Note that if the agent (logical subject) of a passive participle is expressed (examples 3, 4), it is in the instrumental case. In the corresponding relative clause, **котóрый** is in the accusative case, and the logical subject is in the nominative case.

Here are some more examples of synonymous sentence pairs.

В аудитóрию вошёл профéссор, котóрый читáет лéкции по истóрии.
(The professor who lectures on history entered the auditorium.)
В аудитóрию вошёл профéссор, читáющий лéкции по истóрии.
(The professor lecturing on history entered the auditorium.)

Я подошёл к дéвушке, котóрая стоя́ла на автóбусной останóвке.
(I walked up to the young woman who was standing at the bus stop.)
Я подошёл к дéвушке, стоя́вшей на автóбусной останóвке.
(I walked up to the young woman standing at the bus stop.)

Мо́й бра́т знако́м с писа́телем, кото́рый написа́л э́ту кни́гу.
(My brother is acquanited with the writer who wrote this book.)
Мо́й бра́т знако́м с писа́телем, написа́вшим э́ту кни́гу.
(My brother is acquanited with the writer who wrote this book.)

В коридо́ре стоя́т студе́нты, кото́рые сего́дня сдаю́т экза́мены.
(The students who are taking exams today are standing in the hallway.)
В коридо́ре стоя́т студе́нты, сдаю́щие сего́дня экза́мены.
(The students taking exams today are standing in the hallway.)

В на́шей гру́ппе у́чатся студе́нты, кото́рые прие́хали из Кана́ды.
(Students who came from Canada are studying in our group.)
В на́шей гру́ппе у́чатся студе́нты, прие́хавшие из Кана́ды.
(Students coming from Canada are studying in our group.)

In summary, here are some important things to remember about participles.

- participle constructions can only replace **кото́рый** clauses when **кото́рый** is in the nominative or accusative case;
- participles are adjectival forms and agree in case, number and gender with the noun they modify;
- participles do not have a future form.

B. Summary of participle formation

Participles are formed by adding the appropriate endings to the basic verb stem. Here are the basic rules for your reference.

Active Participle		Passive Participle	
Present	Past	Present	Past
1st conj.: **-ущий/-ющий** 2nd conj: **-ащий/-ящий**	After д, т, г, к, б, п, or р:**-ший.** After all others: **-вший.**	1st conj.:**-емый** 2nd conj.: **-имый**	After suffixed stems in -о- and -ну- and after non-suffixed stems in п, м: **-тый.** After suffixed stems in -и- and after non-suffixed (о) stems in б, т, г, к, д, or п: **-енный.** After all others:**-нный.**

	Infinitive	Active Participle		Passive Participle	
		Present	Past	Present	Past
imp.	чита́ть	чита́ющий	чита́вший	чита́емый	—
	открыва́ть	открыва́ющий	открыва́вший	открыва́емый	—
pf.	уви́деть	—	уви́девший	—	уви́денный
	вы́полнить	—	вы́полнивший	—	вы́полненный
	откры́ть	—	откры́вший	—	откры́тый
	сде́лать	—	сде́лавший	—	сде́ланный
imp.	улыба́ться	улыба́ющийся	улыба́вшийся	—	—
pf.	улыбну́ться	—	улыбну́вшийся	—	—

Note that verbs ending in **-ся** follow the same rules for participle formation as those discussed above. However, the particle **-ся** in participles is always spelled **-ся**, never **-сь**, regardless of whether it is preceded by a consonant or a vowel.

Also, only a few verbs have all four participles; some verbs (transitive imperfectives) have three participles; others (transitive perfectives and intransitive imperfectives) have two participles; and still others (intransitive perfectives) have only one participle.

Some participles undergo nominalization, i.e., they can function as nouns as well as adjectives. Note a number of common examples and their English translations.

жела́ющий	interested parties
уча́щийся	student
трудя́щийся	worker

Уро́к 7: Бы́ли ли вы́ на премье́ре?

1. The preposition по

> Я слу́шаю ку́рс по исто́рии ру́сского теа́тра.
> I'm taking a course on the history of Russian theater.

> Спекта́кль по рома́ну Булга́кова бы́л поста́влен в 1977-óм году́.
> The show based on Bulgakov's novel was staged in 1977.

In *Unit 2* the preposition **по** + the dative case is used to denote motion along or around a given place, as in the following examples:

> Мы́ ве́сь ве́чер гуля́ли по Москве́.
> We walked around Moscow all evening.

> Ли́нда и Са́ша ходи́ли по у́лицам и переу́лкам ста́рого Арба́та.
> Linda and Sasha strolled along the streets and lanes of old Arbat (area).

In *Unit 7* you will encounter the following additional meanings of the preposition **по** + the dative case.

A. "On the topic of...(a certain subject)"

По is used with nouns denoting formal subject matter or a specialized area. In this meaning, **по** is usually translated into English as "on."

ку́рс по микробиоло́гии	a course on microbiology
семина́р по исто́рии Росси́и	seminar on the history of Russia
уче́бник по хи́мии	textbook on chemistry
кни́га по совреме́нному иску́сству	a book on modern art

экза́мен по литерату́ре двадца́того ве́ка	an exam on literature of the twentieth century

По also denotes the English phrase, "based on."

фи́льм по рома́ну «Унесённые ве́тром»	a film based on the novel "Gone with the Wind"
спекта́кль по пье́се Шва́рца «Драко́н»	a show based on Shvarts' play "The Dragon"
фи́льм по произведе́ниям Булга́кова	a film based on the works of Bulgakov

B. "According to," "by"

Всё идёт по пла́ну.	Everything is going according to plan.
Поезда́ хо́дят по расписа́нию.	The trains are running according to schedule.

C. По with time periods

Note that with days or other time periods, **по** is always followed by a *plural* noun in the dative case to indicate that something happens regularly at a particular time. (This usage also appears in *Unit 3*.)

У меня́ заня́тия по вто́рникам и четверга́м.
I have classes on Tuesdays and Thursdays.

По вечера́м мы́ обы́чно занима́емся вме́сте.
We usually study together in the evening.

D. Other meanings

Listed below for your reference are examples of some other common uses of **по** + the dative case.

Это мо́й сосе́д (моя́ сосе́дка) по ко́мнате.
This is my roommate.

Это на́ши друзья́ по шко́ле.
These are our friends from school.

Мы́ разгова́ривали по телефо́ну вчера́.
We spoke on the telephone last night.

По телеви́зору сего́дня идёт интере́сный фи́льм.
There is an interesting film on television tonight.

2. Expressing a round trip in past or future: the perfective verbs сходи́ть and съе́здить

Дава́й схо́дим на э́ту вы́ставку!
Let's go to that exhibit!

In *Unit 2,* we used multidirectional, unprefixed verbs of motion (**ходи́ть, е́здить**) in the past tense to express a round trip. Recall that a round trip in the *future* cannot be expressed by an unprefixed verb of motion. Instead, the prefix **с-** is added to a multidirectional verb to create a perfective verb that can express a round trip in the future as well as in the past.

Imperfective	Perfective
ходи́ть	сходи́ть
е́здить	съе́здить[1]

---

[1] Note that there is a hard sign (**ъ**) after the prefix **с-**, and that there is no alternation of **е́зди-** to **езжа́й-**.

A. Round trip in the future

Perfective verbs with the prefix **c-** are the *only way of indicating a round trip in the future.*

Дава́й схо́дим в рестора́н сего́дня ве́чером.
Let's go to a restaurant tonight.

За́втра мы́ обяза́тельно схо́дим на э́ту вы́ставку.
We will definitely go to that exhibit tomorrow.

В суббо́ту я съе́зжу к роди́телям.
I will go visit (make a trip to see) my parents on Saturday.

Когда́ вы́ бу́дете в Петербу́рге, обяза́тельно сходи́те в Эрмита́ж.
When you are in Petersburg, definitely go (make a visit) to the Hermitage.
(**Сходи́ть** *used here in the imperative.*)

Мы́ уже́ ви́дели э́тот спекта́кль. Я ва́м о́чень сове́тую сходи́ть.
We have already seen that show. I highly recommend you go.

B. Past tense

In the past tense, the verbs **сходи́ть** and **съе́здить** differ from **ходи́ть** and **е́здить** in that they indicate that a specific expectation, goal, or intention was fulfilled. Analyze the following examples.

— На́до пойти́ в магази́н. У на́с не́т хле́ба.
"We should go to the grocery store. We don't have any bread."

— Я уже́ сходи́л в магази́н и всё купи́л.
"I already went to the store and bought everything."

— Ка́к ты́ провёл о́тпуск? Хорошо́?
"How did you spend your vacation? Was it good?"

— Да, отли́чно. Я съе́здил в Пари́ж.
"Excellent. I went to Paris."

3. Subordinate clauses with который

> Эта пьеса о добре, которое побеждает зло.
> This play is about goodness, which vanquishes evil.

> В Театре на Таганке мы видели великолепный спектакль «Мастер и Маргарита», в котором Вениамин Смехов играет роль Воланда.
> At the Taganka Theatre we saw the magnificent show, "The Master and Margarita," in which Benjamin Smekhov plays the role of Woland.

Review the formation and use of the relative pronoun **который**, which corresponds to the English "who," "which," or "that." Remember that **который** gets its number and gender from its head noun (antecedent), but its case is determined by its role in the subordinate clause. Also remember that a comma *always precedes* **который**.

> Я ходил(а) в театр с другом, который недавно приехал в Москву.
> I went to the theater with my friend who arrived in Moscow recently.

> Я говорю об актёрах, которые играют в этом спектакле.
> I am talking about the actors who are in that show.

Note the placement and use of prepositions governing **который**.

> Я был(а) на выставке, о которой вы мне рассказывали.
> I have been to the exhibit that (which) you told me about.

> Это дом-музей, в котором жил и работал Достоевский.
> This is the residence-museum in which (where) Dostoevsky lived and worked.

> Вчера мы ходили в галерею, в которой сейчас идёт выставка молодых абстракционистов.
> Yesterday we went to the gallery where currently there is an exhibit of young abstractionists.

Это на́ши бли́зкие друзья́, с кото́рыми мы́ отдыха́ли в про́шлом году́.
These are our close friends with whom we vacationed last year.

4. Дово́лен, дово́льна, дово́льны (че́м): to be pleased/satisfied with

Режиссёр дово́лен на́ми.
The director is pleased with us.

The short-form adjective **дово́лен** (**дово́льна, дово́льно, дово́льны**) is used with a complement in the instrumental case to indicate that the subject is pleased with something or someone. It agrees in number and gender with the subject. Like all short-form adjectives, it can be used only predicatively, and therefore only occurs in the nominative case.

Мы́ всё о́чень дово́льны э́тим ку́рсом.	We are all very pleased with this course.
Ни́на дово́льна свои́м докла́дом.	Nina is pleased with her report.

The past tense is formed by adding **бы́л, была́, бы́ло** or **бы́ли,** also in agreement with the subject.

Он бы́л дово́лен на́шей рабо́той.	He was pleased with our work.
Ма́ма была́ дово́льна свои́ми детьми́.	The mom was pleased with her children.
Они́ бы́ли о́чень дово́льны свое́й пое́здкой.	They were very satisfied with their trip.

The opposite meaning, "dissatisfied, unhappy," can be expressed by adding the prefix **не-** directly to **дово́лен, (дово́льна, дово́льно, дово́льны).**

—Ли́нда, чём ты́ недово́льна?   "What are you dissatisfied (upset) about?"

—Я недово́льна свое́й рабо́той.   "I am dissatisfied with my work."

Худо́жник недово́лен свое́й карти́ной.   The artist is unhappy with his painting.

Студе́нты недово́льны общежи́тием.   The students are unhappy about the dormitory.

To express (dis)satisfacton with something other than a person or thing (i.e., not a noun), the conjunction **то́, что́** is used, with the first element (**то́**) in the instrumental case (**те́м**). English often uses the word "glad" in equivalent statements.

Ли́нда дово́льна **те́м, что́** она́ вы́брала ку́рс по исто́рии ру́сского теа́тра.
Linda is glad that she chose the course on the history of Russian theater.

Все́ дово́льны **те́м, что** мы́ уча́ствовали в спекта́кле.
Everyone is glad that we participated in the show.

5. Overview of verbs of studying, learning and teaching

You have already encountered various verbs related to studying and learning. Provided here is an overview to help you review and systematize your understanding of these verbs.

A. учи́ть/вы́учить что: "to learn, memorize"

Це́лыми дня́ми мы́ все́ учи́ли свои ро́ли.
We spent whole days learning our roles.

The study verb **учи́ть/вы́учить** is encountered again in this unit. Remember that it is a transitive verb that takes a direct object and means "learn," "memorize," and generally implies rote learning of words, memorizing a poem or a part in a play, studying lesson materials, rules, discrete data, etc.

Ди́ма вы́учил всё слова́ пе́сни за оди́н ча́с.
Dima learned all the words of the song in one hour.

Мы́ должны́ учи́ть пра́вила доро́жного движе́ния.
We have to learn the traffic rules.

У на́с за́втра контро́льная по ру́сскому языку́, поэ́тому сего́дня ве́чером я́ бу́ду учи́ть но́вые слова́ и выраже́ния.
We have a quiz tomorrow in Russian, so tonight I am going to study the new words and expressions.

B. учи́ться где́: "to study" (in the sense of "to be a student"); *intransitive; imperfective only*

Remember that when used without an object or infinitive complement, the verb **учи́ться** commonly indicates that one is studying in school, college or university.

—Где́ ты́ у́чишься?
"Where do you go to school (study)?"

Ли́нда у́чится в Моско́вском университе́те.
Linda is studying at Moscow University.

Джо́н у́чится на четвёртом ку́рсе в университе́те.
John is in his fourth year of study at the university.

Ле́том мы́ бу́дем учи́ться на ку́рсах перево́дчиков.
In the summer we will be taking courses (studying) for translators.

C. учи́ться/научи́ться чему́ (or *infinitive*) **у кого́: "to learn, study"**

The verbs of this pair denote learning of any practical and systematic nature: taking dance or music lessons, doing other specialized training, or acquiring a skill or training in a non-academic area.

Дети в этой школе учатся музыке и искусству.
The children in this school study music and art.

Таня научилась играть в шахматы в клубе.
Tanya learned to play chess in the club.

Он учится играть на рояле у знаменитого пианиста.
He is studying piano with a famous pianist.

D. учить/научить кого чему (and/or *infinitive*): "to teach someone something"

The verbs of this pair are generally followed by the *dative* of the subject matter and the *accusative* of the person being taught. The kind of practical, skill-oriented teaching denoted here might be expressed by an English speaker as "to train/teach someone to do something."

Инструктор учит студентов плаванию.
The instructor is teaching the students swimming.

Мой дедушка научил меня вкусно готовить.
My grandfather taught me to cook well.

E. преподавать кому что: "to teach/instruct"; *imperfective only*

The verb **преподавать** takes objects in the *accusative* (denoting subject matter) and *dative* (denoting person(s) being taught). Unlike **учить/научить,** it can stand alone to denote a professional calling.

Том преподаёт английский язык иностранным студентам.
Tom teaches English to foreign students.

Моя́ ма́ма преподаёт хи́мию в колле́дже.
My mother teaches chemistry in college.

—Что́ де́лает ва́ш бра́т?   "What does your brother do?"
—Он преподаёт.   "He teaches."
Моя́ ба́бушка преподава́ла всю́ жи́знь.
My grandmother taught all her life.

Я хочу́ преподава́ть в сре́дней шко́ле.
I want to teach in grade school.

F. изуча́ть/изучи́ть что́: "to study," "to learn," "to investigate"

The verbs of this pair, which are *always* followed by an object in the accusative case, denote thorough and deep study of a subject area or discipline. They are often used in reference to graduate study and professional-level investigation.

Социо́логи изуча́ют пробле́мы больши́х городо́в.
Sociologists are studying the problems of big cities.

В аспиранту́ре я изуча́л математи́ческую ло́гику.
In graduate school I studied mathematical logic.

Гео́логи изуча́ют измене́ния в кли́мате.
Geologists are studying the changes in climate.

Я сейча́с пишу́ диссерта́цию. Я изуча́ю пробле́мы эколо́гии.
I am currently writing my dissertation. I am studying ecological problems.

G. занима́ться че́м: "to study," "to be occupied with," "to major in"

This intransitive verb denotes participation in a wide range of academic, vocational, and avocational pursuits. It is the usual way of conveying the idea of "majoring" at the undergraduate level. It occurs with an instrumental complement (see *Unit 1*) to express one's interests, hobbies and leisure activities (see *Unit 9*).

Джо́н занима́ется би́знесом.
John studies business.

Я занима́юсь ру́сским языко́м.
I study Russian.
Мы́ занима́емся спо́ртом ка́ждый де́нь.
We participate in sports everyday.

Ли́нда занима́ется бе́гом уже́ не́сколько ле́т.
Linda has been jogging for a few years already.

This verb, when used without an object, is the Russian equivalent of the English "to be studying."

— Что́ ты́ сейча́с де́лаешь? — "What are you doing now?"
— Я занима́юсь. — "I'm studying."

— Что́ ты́ де́лал(а) вчера́ ве́чером? "What did you do last night?"
— Я сиде́л(а) до́ма и занима́лся (занима́лась). "I stayed home and studied."

— Каки́е у тебя́ пла́ны на выходны́е? "What are your plans for the weekend?"
— Я бу́ду занима́ться. "I'll be studying."

6. The superlative degree of adjectives and adverbs

Спекта́кль «Ма́стер и Маргари́та» — са́мый популя́рный спекта́кль Теа́тра на Тага́нке.
The show "The Master and Margarita" is the most popular show of the Taganka Theater.

A. The superlative degree of adjectives

The superlative degree of both long- and short-form adjectives is formed by placing the *declinable* word са́мый before the positive degree of the adjective. Like any adjective, it must agree in case, gender, and number with the noun it modifies.

По-мо́ему, э́то са́мая интере́сная карти́на на вы́ставке.
In my opinion, this is the most interesting painting in the exhibit.

«Славя́нка» — э́то са́мый дорого́й рестора́н в Москве́.
"Slavyanka" is the most expensive restaurant in Moscow.

Мо́й са́мый люби́мый актёр — Шо́н Ко́ннери.
My favorite actor is Sean Connery.

На́ш до́м нахо́дится в са́мой ста́рой ча́сти го́рода.
Our house is located in the oldest part of the city.

Э́та актри́са о́чень популя́рная. Она́ игра́ет в моём са́мом люби́мом фи́льме.
That actress is very popular. She plays in my favorite film.

Recall the superlatives for the following adjectives:

Positive Degree		Simple Comparative		Superlative	
хоро́ший	good	лу́чше	better	лу́чший	best
плохо́й	bad	ху́же	worse	ху́дший	worst

To describe "the least...," use the word **наиме́нее** + the positive degree of the adjective.

Э́то наиме́нее интере́сная карти́на на вы́ставке.
This is the least interesting painting in the exhibit.

B. Synthetic superlative

The synthetic superlative, which consists of the simple comparative followed by either **всех** or **всего́**, is very common in spoken Russian. This form can be used only predicatively, i.e., when a simple comparative is possible[1].

Са́ша моло́же всех.
Sasha is the youngest (of all).

Эта карти́на интере́снее всех.
This painting is the most interesting one (more interesting than all the others).

Национа́льная галере́я бога́че всех остальны́х музе́ев.
The National Gallery is richer than all the other museums.

This is also the way to form a superlative adverb.

Ли́нда говори́т по-ру́сски лу́чше всех.
Linda speaks Russian best of all (better than anyone).

Бо́льше всего́ я люблю́ чита́ть.
I love to read more than anything.

Оля бе́гает быстре́е всех.
Olya runs faster than anyone.

7. Passive constructions using short-form verbal adjectives (participles)

Теа́тр на Тага́нке был со́здан в нача́ле шестидеся́тых годо́в тала́нтливым режиссёром Ю́рием Петро́вичем Люби́мовым.

The Taganka Theater was founded in the early sixties by the talented director Yury Petrovich Lubimov.

This form is no longer productive in modern Russian and exists only for a few adjectives typically used in academic and topical writing. In other speech styles, such forms are used as elatives or "absolutesuperlatives," i.e., without any comparison with other persons or objects. There are many set phrases containing such forms (e.g. кратча́йший путь "shortest way," ближа́йшая остано́вка "nearest stop," крупне́йший писа́тель "eminent writer.") They are also used in scholarly writing (e.g. нове́йшая исто́рия "very recent history," мельча́йшие дета́ли "minute details.")

A. Usage

You already know that a passive meaning can be conveyed by the third-person plural form of a transitive verb with no subject.

Теа́тр на Тага́нке **со́здали** в нача́ле шестидеся́тых годо́в.
The Taganka Theater was founded in the early sixties.

Another way to express the passive is to use a short-form past passive verbal adjective. These verbal adjectives function as predicates or parts of predicates; i.e. they are only possible in the nominative case and agree with the subject of the sentence or clause. They ascribe to the subject the quality of the action undergone. This form is very common in conversational Russian.

Compare the following examples of how a passive meaning can be conveyed in Russian.

Third-person verb without a stated subject	Short-form passive verbal adjectives
Ско́ро откро́ют э́ту вы́ставку.	Э́та вы́ставка ско́ро бу́дет откры́та.

This exhibit will soon be opened.

Петербу́рг постро́или в нача́ле XVIII ве́ка.	Петербу́рг бы́л постро́ен в нача́ле XVIII ве́ка.

Petersburg was built in the beginning of the XVIII century.

Compare the following pairs of active and passive sentences, noting the grammatical cases in which the subject and object are expressed. In the active constructions, the subject is in the nominative and the object in the accusative. In passive constructions, however, the object of the active sentence becomes the grammatical subject of the passive construction, and the agent performing the action is in the instrumental case.

Active	Passive
Михаи́л Булга́ков написа́л рома́н «Ма́стер и Маргари́та».	Рома́н «Ма́стер и Маргари́та» напи́сан Михаи́лом Булга́ковым.
Mikhail Bulgakov wrote the novel, "The Master and Margarita."	The novel "The Master and Margarita" was written by Mikhail Bulgakov.
Ломоно́сов со́здал Моско́вский университе́т.	Моско́вский университе́т со́здан Ломоно́совым.
Lomonosov founded Moscow University.	Moscow University was founded by Lomonosov.
Марша́к перевёл стихи́ Ро́берта Бёрнса на ру́сский язы́к.	Стихи́ Ро́берта Бёрнса переведены́ на ру́сский язы́к Марша́ком.
Marshak translated Robert Burns' poems into Russian.	Robert Burns' poems were translated into Russian by Marshak.

B. Formation

Short-form past passive verbal adjectives are formed in the same way as their long-form counterparts (see *Unit 6*), but they have short- rather than long-form endings. At this stage of study, you are not expected to be able to *form* short-form passive participles. You should, however, be able to recognize them and understand their function. Here is a table summarizing the forms that appear in *Unit 7*. These are among those most commonly encountered in spoken Russian, and therefore should be memorized.

Infinitive	Stem	Short-form passive verbal adjective	Meaning
созда́ть	созда́ть (irreg.)	со́здан, со́здана, со́здано, со́зданы	to be founded
поста́вить	поста́ви-	поста́влен, поста́влена, поста́влено, поста́влены	to be staged
написа́ть	написа-ˣ	напи́сан, напи́сана, напи́сано, напи́саны	to be written

перевести	*перевёд-*	переведён, переведена, переведено, переведены	to be translated
построить	*построи-*	построен, построена, построено, построены	to be built
открыть	*открой-*	открыт, открыта, открыто, открыты	to be opened
закрыть	*закрой-*	закрыт, закрыта, закрыто, закрыты	to be closed
нарисовать	*нарисовá-*	нарисован, нарисована, нарисовано, нарисованы	to be drawn
сделать	*сделай-*	сделан, сделана, сделано, сделаны	to be done, made
собрать	*соб/рá-*ˣ	собран, собрана, собрано, собраны	to be collected
решить	*реши-*	решён, решена, решено, решены	to be decided
продать	*продáть* (irreg.)	продан, продана, продано, проданы	to be sold

8. Summary and review: long- and short-form adjectives

The following is a list of commonly used short-form adjectives appearing throughout *Russian Stage 2*.

рáд(а) познакóмиться	pleased to meet you (Unit 1)
знакóм(а) с кéм	be acquainted with, know someone (Unit 1)
зáнят(а)/свобóден (свобóдна) пóсле пятú	busy/free after five (Unit 3)
óн похóж на мáму (пáпу)	he looks like mama (papa) (Unit 4)
ýжин готóв	dinner is ready (Unit 6)

я уже́ сы́т (сыта́)	I am already full (Unit 6)
режиссёр дово́лен на́ми	the director is pleased with us (Unit 7)
Ли́нда больна́/здоро́ва	Linda is sick/healthy (Unit 8)
о́н уве́рен, она́ уве́рена	he is sure, she is sure (Unit 8)
ви́ден ве́сь го́род	the whole city is visible (Unit 10)
мы́ с ва́ми согла́сны	you and I agree (Unit 10)

You have learned them primarily as lexical (vocabulary) items. The explanation that follows is a more systematic overview of the formation and function of short-form adjectives.

Most Russian adjectives denoting *qualities* have two forms: the short form and the long form. The long form is used *attributively* to qualify nouns and also *predicatively* (as a "predicate adjective"), usually after the verb **бы́ть**. The short form, on the other hand, is used *only* as all or part of a predicate.

Short-form adjectives are formed by adding the appropriate gender markers to the stem of the long-form adjective: -ø (*masc.*), **-а/-я** (*fem.*), and **о/-е** (*neut.*) and the plural ending **-ы/-и** (for all genders). Past and future tense predicates are formed by using the appropriate form of the verb **бы́ть** in agreement with the subject.

A. Usage of short-form adjectives

There are several groups of short-form adjectives that have no long-form counterparts *with the same meaning*. These adjectives occur in all speech styles of the spoken and the written language. Here are some examples.

1. Some adjectives exist *only* in the short form.

до́лжен, должна́, должно́, должны́ Мы́ должны́ позвони́ть Оле́гу.	"be obligated, should" We should call Oleg.
ра́д, ра́да, ра́до, ра́ды	"be happy"

Я ра́д(а) с ва́ми познако́миться.   I am happy to meet you.

2. Some adjectives have short forms with a meaning different from their long-form counterparts. Generally, the short forms are highly bound to a particular context, time, etc. and express temporary or relational qualities; whereas the long-forms tend to describe permanent features, and can be used predicatively or attributively. Study the following examples.

ви́ден, видна́, ви́дно, видны́   **ви́дный**
Отсю́да ви́ден весь го́род.   На ви́дном ме́сте стои́т па́мятник.
The whole city is visible from here.   The monument stands in a visible place.

жив, жива́, жи́во, жи́вы   **живо́й**
Моя́ прабабушка ещё жива́.   Он о́чень живо́й челове́к.
My great-grandmother is still alive.   He is a very lively person.

здоро́в, здоро́ва, здоро́во, здоро́вы   **здоро́вый**
Ли́нда боле́ла, но сейча́с она́ здоро́ва.   Он о́чень здоро́вый челове́к.
Linda was sick, but she's better now.   He is a very healthy person.

прав, права́, пра́во, пра́вы   **пра́вый**
Вы соверше́нно пра́вы в э́той ситуа́ции.   Это пра́вое де́ло.
You are absolutely right (correct) in this   This is a just cause.
situation.

свобо́ден, свобо́дна, свобо́дно, свобо́дны   **свобо́дный**

Мы свобо́дны сего́дня по́сле пяти́.   Всё своё свобо́дное вре́мя он
                                                 проводит в клу́бе.
We are free tonight after five.   He spends all his free time at the club.

сыт, сыта́, сы́то, сы́ты   **сы́тый**
Я уже́ сыт(а́).   Сы́тый (челове́к) голо́дного не
                                                 разуме́ет. (*proverb*)
I am already full (of food).   A full person doesn't understand a
                                                 hungry one.

Many of these short-form adjectives are capable of syntactic government, i.e. they require a certain case with or without a preposition.

бо́лен, больна́, больно́, больны́ (че́м)
Её сего́дня не бу́дет. Она́ больна́.
She won't be here today. She is sick.

больно́й
Наш де́душка больно́й челове́к.
Our grandfather is an ill man.

винова́т, винова́та, винова́то, винова́ты (в че́м)
Я ни в чём не винова́т.
I am not guilty of anything.

винова́тый

У него́ винова́тый ви́д.
He has a guilty look (appearance).

гото́в, гото́ва, гото́во, гото́вы (к чему́)
Мы́ бу́дем гото́вы через пя́ть мину́т.

We will be ready in five minutes.

гото́вый
В э́том магази́не мо́жно купи́ть гото́вые блю́да.
You can buy prepared foods in this store.

дово́лен, дово́льна, дово́льно, дово́льны (че́м, ке́м)
Преподава́тель дово́лен на́ми.
The teacher is pleased with us.

дово́льный

У неё о́чень дово́льный ви́д.
She has a very pleased (satisfied) look.

жена́т (на ко́м)
Ива́н жена́т на Оле.
Ivan is married to Olya.

жена́тый
Он жена́тый челове́к.
He is a married man.

за́мужем[1] (за ке́м)
Оля за́мужем за Ива́ном.
Olya is married to Ivan.

заму́жняя
Оля за́мужняя же́нщина.
Olya is a married woman.

---

[1] Note that the form **за́мужем** is used to refer to a woman, even though it lacks a feminine ending. It is actually derived from за + instrumental of **му́ж = за́мужем**.

за́нят, занята́, за́нято, за́няты (че́м)
Мы́ бы́ли за́няты вчера́ ве́чером.

We were busy last night.

знако́м, знако́ма, знако́мо
знако́мы (с ке́м) (незнако́м с ке́м)
Мы́ с ни́м знако́мы давно́.

We have known each other for a long time.

похо́ж, похо́жа, похо́же,
похо́жи (на что́, на кого́)
Сы́н похо́ж на отца́.
The son looks like the father.

согла́сен, согла́сна, согла́сно,
согла́сны (с ке́м, с че́м)
Мы́ с ва́ми согла́сны.
You and I agree.

уве́рен, уве́рена, уве́рено,
уве́рены (в че́м)
Я́ уве́рен в э́том.
I am certain (confident) of that.

занято́й
На́ш профе́ссор о́чень за́нятый челове́к.
Our professor is a very busy person.

знако́мый

У неё о́чень знако́мое лицо́, но я́ её не по́мню.
She has a very familiar face, but I don't remember her.

похо́жий

У ни́х похо́жие хара́ктеры.
They have similar personalities.

согла́сный[1]

уве́ренный

У него́ уве́ренный ви́д.
He has a confident appearance.

Also in this group are adjectives whose short forms have the meaning of "excessiveness" (e.g. *too* big, *too* small). These are often used in referring to sizes of clothing and dimensions.

широ́к, широка́, широко́, широки́

too wide
Этот га́лстук сли́шком широ́к.
That tie is too wide.

---

[1] This long-form adjective is outdated and no longer used.

ко́роток, коротка́, ко́ротко, ко́ротки	too short Эта ю́бка мне́ коротка́. This skirt is too short for me.
у́зок, узка́, у́зко, узки́	too narrow Эти ту́фли узки́. These shoes are too narrow.
вели́к, велика́, велико́, велики́	too big Этот костю́м ва́м вели́к. That suit is too big for you.
ма́л, мала́, мало́, малы́	too small Эти джи́нсы мне́ малы́. These jeans are too small for me.
дли́нен, длинна́, длинно́, длинны́	too long Это пла́тье мне́ немно́жко длинно́. This dress is a little bit too long for me.

3. There are some constructions where only short-form adjectives can be used, e.g., with the imperative of verbs.

Бу́дьте добры́,....	Please be so kind,....
Бу́дьте внима́тельны,....	Be careful (mindful)....
Бу́дьте любе́зны,....	Please be so kind,....
Бу́дьте здоро́вы!	Be healthy! (Also used when someone sneezes to say, "Gesundheit!")

Important note: Short-form adjectives do not combine with the pronoun **тако́й** (such) or **како́й** (what kind), but rather with the adverbs **та́к** (so) or **ка́к** (how).

Она́ та́к больна́, что не выхо́дит
из до́ма.
She is so sick that she isn't leaving
the house.

Он тако́й больно́й челове́к!
He is such a sick person!

Он сего́дня бы́л та́к за́нят, что да́же
не успе́л пообе́дать
He was so busy today, that he didn't
even manage to eat lunch.

Мы́ таки́е за́нятые лю́ди, что́
у на́с совсе́м не́т свобо́дного вре́мени.
We are such busy people, that we don't
have any free time.

Он та́к дово́лен студе́нтами, что́ о́н
отмени́л экза́мен.
He is so pleased with the students that
he cancelled the exam.

У него́ тако́й дово́льный ви́д!
He has such a satisfied look!

B. Formation of short-form adjectives

A long-form adjective stem ending in a consonant preceded by a vowel remains unchanged:
счастли́вый — сча́стлив. A long-form adjective stem ending in two consonants changes
in masculine short-form, where the vowel **o** or **e** is inserted between the two consonants:
коро́ткий — коро́ток, у́зкий — у́зок. (Stems ending in -ст- constitute an exception to
this rule.) Study the following chart.

	Masculine	*Feminine*	*Neuter*	*Plural*
интере́сн-ый	интере́сен	интере́сна	интере́сно	интере́сны
прекра́сн-ый	прекра́сен	прекра́сна	прекра́сно	прекра́сны
краси́в-ый	краси́в	краси́ва	краси́во	краси́вы
хоро́ш-ий	хоро́ш	хороша́	хорошо́	хоро́ши
прост-о́й	про́ст	проста́	про́сто	просты́
коро́тк-ий	ко́роток	коротка́	ко́ротко	ко́ротки
у́зк-ий	у́зок	узка́	у́зко	узки́

Note the stress shift in the feminine forms of the last two adjectives in the chart: the stress is shifted to the final **-а**. Note also: **ма́л, мала́, мало́, малы́.**

No short-form adjectives can be derived from long-form adjectives ending in **-ск(ий)** or **-ов(ой)** (e.g., дру́жеский, делово́й). Also, many long-form adjectives that have appeared in the language comparatively recently have no short forms.

Уро́к 8: Ка́к вы́ себя́ чу́вствуете?

1. Discussing health

> Уже́ два́ дня́ я боле́ю.
> I have been sick for two days already.
>
> Ната́ша говори́т, что́ я́ заболе́ла, потому́ что я́ ходи́ла без пальто́ и ша́пки.
> Natasha says that I got sick because I didn't wear a coat and hat.

> Сего́дня я́ чу́вствую себя́ лу́чше, у меня́ уже́ норма́льная
> температу́ра, го́рло почти́ не боли́т.
> Today I feel better, my temperature is already back to normal,
> and my throat almost doesn't hurt at all.

Study the following constructions used in Russian to discuss health.

A. боле́ть/заболе́ть *(note stem: боле́й-)*: **"to be sick"**

This verb is intransitive (i.e., it cannot take a direct object). The perfective indicates the *onset* of illness.

Уже́ два́ дня́ я́ боле́ю.
I have been sick for two days already.

Ната́ша говори́т, что́ я́ заболе́ла, потому́ что я́ ходи́ла без пальто́ и ша́пки.
Natasha says that I got sick because I didn't wear (*lit.* walked around without) a coat and hat.

This verb can also take an instrumental complement.

Чём вы́ боле́ете?	What (illness) do you have?
Она́ боле́ет гри́ппом.	She has the flu.
Он боле́ет анги́ной.	He has a sore throat.

B. Using a construction of possession to specify an ailment

In Russian, just as in English, you can use a construction of possession to specify someone's ailment (e.g. "I *have* a cold.")

> **y** + the person who is sick (genitive) + the ailment (nominative)

Note that **éсть** is always omitted in the present tense.

> Серге́я сего́дня не бу́дет. Он боле́ет. У него́ гри́пп.
> Sergey won't be here today. He is sick. He has the flu.
>
> Я лежа́л(а) до́ма на про́шлой неде́ле. Я тяжело́ боле́л(а). У меня́ бы́л
> како́й-то ви́рус.
> I was at home in bed last week. I was terribly sick. I had some sort of virus.

C. чу́вствовать себя́: "to feel..."; *imperfective only*

The verb **чу́вствовать (себя́)** is used to state or ask how someone feels. The word **себя́** cannot be omitted when expressing this meaning.

> — Ка́к вы́ себя́ чу́вствуете? — "How do you feel?"
> — Спаси́бо, я́ чу́вствую себя́ — "Thanks, I feel better (fine, awful)."
> лу́чше (хорошо́, пло́хо).

D. болеть *(note stem:* болé-*)*: **"to hurt," "to ache"**; *imperfective only*

This imperfective verb is used to express that something aches. It is only used in the third person. Its infinitive is identical to the infinitive form for the verb meaning "to be sick": **болéть** (болéй-); however, note that these two verbs have *different basic stems* (болéй- is a first-conjugation verb; болé- is a second-conjugation verb).

У меня́ боли́т голова́. (У меня́ вчера́ болéла голова́.)
I have a headache (my head aches). (I had a headache yesterday.)

У отца́ постоя́нно боля́т нóги.
Father's legs ache/hurt constantly.

Гóрло почти́ не боли́т.
My throat barely hurts anymore.

Я сидéл(а) за компью́тером цéлый день, и у меня́ сейча́с боли́т спина́.
I sat at the computer all day, and now my back aches.

Note again the use of the **у** + genitive construction of possession in the examples above.

E. Он бóлен, она́ больна́, они́ больны́

Another way to say that someone is sick is to use this short-form adjective. These forms are used only predicatively (and therefore only in the nominative), and they agree in gender and number with the subject. Past and future are formed by adding the appropriate form of **быть** to agree with the subject. Remember that the long-form adjective **больнóй** means "to be sickly" in general.

— Па́вел был с ва́ми на экску́рсии?   "Was Pavel with you on the excursion?"

— Нéт, он тогда́ был бóлен.   "No, he was sick then."

— А ка́к он сейча́с себя́ чу́вствует?   "How does he feel now?"

— Хорошó. Сейча́с он здорóв.   "Fine. He's fine now."

2. Describing the weather

Both personal and impersonal constructions can be used to discuss the weather in Russian. The following examples show how you can use the subject **погóда** with a variety of adjectives and verbs.

— Какáя сегóдня погóда?	"What is the weather like today?"
— Сегóдня отлúчная погóда!	"It's excellent!"
— Какáя былá погóда на юге?	"What was the weather like down south?"
— На юге былá плохáя погóда.	"It was awful weather down south."
— Какáя бýдет погóда зáвтра?	"What will the weather be like tomorrow?"
— Зáвтра бýдет тёплая погóда.	"It will be warm tomorrow."

У нáс в Вашингтóне в áвгусте всегдá ужáсная, жáркая погóда.
In Washington we always have horrible, hot weather in August.

Impersonal constructions are also commonly used to discuss the weather. In these sentences, there is no nominative subject. Note that English requires a subject, and most often uses "it" in cases where Russian uses an impersonal construction.

— Кáк сегóдня на ýлице?	"What is it like out today?"
— Сегóдня на ýлице теплó.	"Today it is warm."
(хóлодно, жáрко, прекрáсно)	(cold, hot, beautiful)

Sometimes just the predicate is stated in conversational style speech.

— Кáк сегóдня на ýлице?	"What is it like out today?"
— Теплó. (жáрко, влáжно, прохлáдно)	"(It is) warm." (hot, humid, cool)

As with all impersonal constructions, the neuter singular form of the verb **быть** is added to express future or past.

> Мы́ гуля́ли в Изма́йлове до́лго, бы́ло тепло́.
> We spent a long time wandering around Izmailovo, it was warm.

> Вчера́ бы́ло тепло́, а сего́дня хо́лодно.
> It was warm yesterday, but it is cold today.

> За́втра бу́дет прохла́дно.
> It will be cold tomorrow.

> Когда́ мы́ бы́ли в Москве́, бы́ло о́чень хо́лодно.
> When we were in Moscow, it was very cold!

In the following examples, note how **кака́я** and **така́я** are used when the noun **пого́да** is stated; whereas in impersonal constructions, **ка́к** and **та́к** are used.

> Сего́дня така́я хоро́шая пого́да!
> The weather is so nice today!

> Сего́дня та́к хорошо́ на у́лице!
> It is so nice outside today!

> Вчера́ бы́ло та́к хо́лодно, что мы́ гуля́ли недо́лго.
> It was so cold yesterday that we didn't stay outside very long.

A change in weather can be expressed by using an impersonal construction with the neuter singular form of the verb **ста́ть** "become."

> Но́ когда́ мы́ шли́ обра́тно, ста́ло хо́лодно, и я́ о́чень замёрзла.
> But when we were on our way back, it got cold and I really froze.

Simple comparatives can also serve as the predicates in such impersonal constructions.

> Вчерá бы́ло хóлодно, а сегóдня теплée.
> It was cold yesterday, but it is warmer today.

> Сегóдня идёт дóждь, но зáвтра бýдет лýчше.
> It is raining today, but it will be nicer tomorrow.

Recall the idiomatic use of the verb **идти́** to say that it is raining or snowing.

Идёт дóждь.	It's raining.
Шёл дóждь. Бýдет идти́ дóждь.	It was raining. It's going to rain.
Идёт снéг.	It's snowing.
Шёл снéг. Бýдет идти́ снéг.	It was snowing. It's going to snow.

The verb **пойти́** is used to indicate the onset of rain or snow.

> Когдá мы́ éхали домóй, пошёл дóждь.
> When we were on our way home, it started to rain.

> Пойдём быстрée отсю́да. Сейчáс пойдёт дóждь.
> Let's get out of here fast. It's about to start raining.

3. Simultaneous vs. consecutive actions and aspect[1]

Recall that the imperfective aspect is used to indicate that more than one action is occuring (did or will occur) *simultaneously*. In contrast, the perfective aspect is used to indicate that more than one action did or will occur *consecutively*, each action being completed before the next one is begun. Study the following examples.

---

[1] See also *Unit 3*.

Вчера́ ве́чером я́ убира́л(а) ко́мнату и слу́шал(а) му́зыку.
Last night I cleaned my room and listened to music (at the same time).
(*simultaneous actions*)

Ли́нда сняла́ зи́мнее пальто́ и пове́сила в шка́ф, убрала́ тёплые зи́мние
сапоги́.
Linda took off her winter coat and hung it in the closet, (then) she put away
her warm winter boots. (*sequence of actions*)

Вра́ч до́лго осма́тривал меня́ и спра́шивал, что́ у меня́ боли́т.
The doctor was examining me for a long time while asking me what was
hurting. (*simultaneous actions*)

Вра́ч посмотре́л го́рло, послу́шал лёгкие и се́рдце и сказа́л, что у
меня́ грипп.
The doctor examined my throat, (then) he examined my lungs and heart, and
(then) he said that I had the flu. (*sequence of actions*)

4. The conjunctions поэ́тому and потому́ что

Ната́ша говори́т, что́ я́ заболе́ла, потому́ что я́ ходи́ла без пальто́ и ша́пки.
Natasha says that I got sick because I didn't wear a coat and hat.

The conjunctions **поэ́тому** ("therefore; that's why") and **потому́ что** ("because") are used
throughout *Unit 8* to join two clauses and indicate a causal relationship. Review their usage,
noting that they are both always preceded by commas.

Он не пришёл на репети́цию, потому́ что заболе́л.
He didn't come to rehearsal because he got sick.

Он заболе́л, поэ́тому о́н не пришёл на репети́цию.
He got sick and therefore (that's why) he didn't come to rehearsal.

5. Clauses of purpose introduced by чтóбы

In *Unit 8* you have been using **чтóбы** with a verb in the past tense to report commands, requests, and wishes[1], as in the following example.

> Врáч сказáл, чтóбы я́ полоскáла гóрло, пилá лекáрство и лежáла три́ дня́.
> The doctor told me to gargle, take my medicine, and stay in bed for three days.

Remember that **чтóбы** is also used to introduce subordinate clauses of purpose. Two different grammatical structures are possible:

1. When the subjects of the two clauses are the same, use **чтóбы + infinitive**.

Я́ зашёл в аптéку, чтóбы купи́ть лекáрство.
I stopped by the pharmacy to (in order to/so that I could) buy medicine.

English often uses only an infinitive, but in Russian **чтóбы** is generally not omitted. If "in order to" can be inserted into the English equivalent expression, **чтобы** should be used in Russian.

2. When the subjects of the two clauses are different, use **чтобы + past tense**.

Я́ зашёл к врачу́, чтóбы óн вы́писал рецéпт.
I stopped by the doctor's *so that he* could write (me) a prescription.

6. "If... then...." clauses expressing real conditions

> Éсли зáвтра я́ бýду себя́ чýвствовать хорошó, я́ обязáтельно пойдý гуля́ть.
> If I feel better tomorrow, I will definitely go out for a walk.

---

[1] See *Unit 1 #8* on reported speech.

The conjunction **éсли** (if) is used to introduce a real condition. When the main (consequence) clause follows the "if"-clause, it may or may not be introduced by **тó** (then); just as in English, this second conjunction is often omitted.

In the following examples, contrast the tenses of the Russian and English "if"-clauses. Note that Russian is much more specific in preserving the actual tense of the action in the "if"-clause if it is presumed to be in the future, whereas English uses present tense.

> Если за́втра бу́дет хо́лодно, (тó) мы́ не пое́дем на́ пля́ж.
> If it's (*will be*) cold tomorrow, (then) we won't go to the beach.

> Если вы́ не ви́дели э́тот фи́льм, (тó) обяза́тельно сходи́те.
> If you have never seen that film, (then) definitely go.

> Если у меня́ бу́дут де́ньги, я́ обяза́тельно пое́ду в Евро́пу э́тим ле́том.
> If I (*will*) have the money, I will definitely go to Europe this summer.

7. The subjunctive mood

> Если бы я́ оде́лась тепле́е, я́ бы не заболе́ла.
>
> If I had dressed more warmly (*but I didn't*), I wouldn't have gotten sick (*but I did*).

To indicate that an action or condition is hypothetical, contrary to fact, "irreal," or highly unlikely, Russian uses the unstressed particle **бы**, often (but not always) in conjunction with **éсли**. The particle **бы** and the word immediately preceding it are pronounced as a single unit. The particle **бы** is placed either after the first stressed element in the sentence or immediately after the verb. Grammatically, **бы** requires that the verb be in the past tense; thus, the actual tense of the utterance can be determined only by context.

> Если бы о́н мне́ позвони́л, я́ бы ему́ сказа́л(а) об э́том.
> If he had called me (*but he didn't*), I would have told him about that (*but I didn't*).

> О́н бы пошёл за́втра на заня́тия, е́сли бы не́ был бо́лен.
> He would go to classes tomorrow (*but he won't*) if he weren't sick (*but he is*).

Мы́ бы пошли́ за́втра ве́чером с ва́ми в теа́тр, е́сли бы у на́с бы́ли биле́ты.
We would go with you to the theatre tomorrow night (*but we won't*), if we had tickets (*but we don't*).

Note that when the particle **бы** is used in a sentence that does not contain a condition, it indicates that the action is desirable[1] . This use of **бы** "softens" the utterance and makes it sound more polite.

— Вы́ что́-нибудь хоти́те пи́ть?   "Would you like something to drink?"
— Я бы́ вы́пил(а) стака́н воды́.   "I would like (*lit.* I would drink) a glass of
water."

Я бы о́чень хоте́ла пойти́ с ва́ми на э́тот спекта́кль. Мо́жно ещё доста́ть биле́ты?
I would love to go to that show with you. Can you still get tickets?

---

[1] This use of **бы** is not included in this unit.

Уро́к 9: Че́м вы́ увлека́етесь? Что́ ва́с интересу́ет?

1. Expressing interests: занима́ться, увлека́ться, интересова́ться

> Я занима́юсь бе́гом уже́ не́сколько ле́т.
> I have been jogging for a few years already.
>
> В Москве́ мно́гие увлека́ются бе́гом.
> Many people in Moscow like to jog.
>
> Ната́ша интересу́ется фотогра́фией.
> Natasha is interested in photography.

The verbs **занима́ться, увлека́ться,** and **интересова́ться** are used to express interests, hobbies, and pastimes. They all require an instrumental complement.

Занима́ться refers to an activity that the subject actually participates in. This verb is often used in connection with sports activities and indicates that the subject is not merely a fan, but actually plays the sport. As you have seen, it also means "to study," or literally, "to occupy oneself" with a given subject.

> Он занима́ется пла́ванием всю́ жи́знь. Он о́чень хорошо́ пла́вает.
> He has been (engaging in) swimming all his life. He swims very well.
>
> Она́ занима́ется му́зыкой. Она́ игра́ет на скри́пке и на роя́ле.
> She studies music. She plays both the violin and the piano.

Интересова́ться, "to be interested in," has a more passive meaning. For example, the sentence «**Она́ занима́ется жи́вописью**» means that she actually draws or paints herself, whereas the sentence «**Она́ интересу́ется жи́вописью**» means that she is interested in painting, but she may not necessarily draw herself.

Ли́нда интересу́ется совреме́нными фи́льмами.
Linda is interested in contemporary films.

Джо́н интересу́ется исто́рией.
John is interested in history. (*He's a history buff.*)

Я интересу́юсь класси́ческой му́зыкой.
I am interested in classical music. (*This says nothing about whether or not I myself am a musician/composer.*)

Увлека́ться is close to the English "to love something," "to be an avid fan of something."

Бори́с увлека́ется му́зыкой.
Boris loves music.

Они́ увлека́ются та́нцами.
They love dancing.

2. Multi-directional verbs of motion to describe a general activity

Throughout *Unit 9*, multi-directional verbs of motion are used to describe a generic, regular activity. (You have seen this before, in *Unit 2* and elsewhere.) The following examples give you a chance to review this meaning, as well as the forms of multi-directional verbs.

ходи́ть (ходи́-): to walk

У меня́ нет маши́ны. Я всегда́ хожу́ пешко́м.
I don't have a car. I always walk.

Та́ня уме́ет ходи́ть на лы́жах.
Tanya knows how to ski.

бе́гать (бе́гай-): to run, jog

Я о́чень люблю́ бе́гать. Я бе́гаю ка́ждое у́тро.
I really love to jog. I jog every morning.

éздить (éзди-): to ride

> Ра́ньше я́ ча́сто éздил(а) на велосипéде, а сейча́с совсéм не éзжу.
> I used to bicycle (to ride a bike) often, but I don't do it at all now.

пла́вать (пла́вай-): to swim

> Ди́ме то́лько три́ го́да, а о́н ужé умéет пла́вать.
> Dima is only three years old and he already knows how to swim.

3. Imperfective infinitives after certain verbs

> В дéтстве я́ то́же собира́ла ма́рки, но пото́м мнé надоéло собира́ть ма́рки, и я́ начала́ собира́ть откры́тки, но бро́сила и э́то.
>
> In childhood I also collected stamps, but then I got sick of collecting stamps and started collecting postcards, but I quit doing that, too.

Throughout *Russian Stage 2*, particularly in *Unit 3*, you have encountered certain verbs that by definition emphasize *process and activity,* and which are therefore logically followed by an *imperfective* infinitive. Here are some that you already know.

начина́ть/нача́ть	begin
конча́ть/ко́нчить	end
продолжа́ть/продо́лжить	continue
станови́ться/ста́ть	begin
переста́ва́ть/переста́ть	cease, stop
учи́ться/научи́ться	learn
нра́виться/понра́виться	like

The following verbs introduced in *Unit 9* also belong to this group. These verbs indicate the subject's *attitude* toward a given activity, and in no way signify result or completion.

уставáть/устáть	grow tired (of)
привыкáть/привы́кнуть	get accustomed to
отвыкáть/отвы́кнуть	get out of the habit of
бросáть/брóсить	quit
надоедáть/надоéсть	be (sick and) tired of

Learn the meanings and conjugations for these verbs. Remember that the (**ну-**) suffix, when in brackets, indicates that **-ну-** disappears in the past tense: **óн привы́к, онá привы́кла, они́ привы́кли.**

A special note about the verb **надоедáть/надоéсть**: this verb functions much like **нрáвится/понрáвиться.** The logical subject is expressed in the *dative* case. If the thing that the subject has grown sick of is an *activity*, then this activity is expressed by an imperfective infinitive; if it is a noun, then this noun is in the *nominative* case. Like the verb **уставáть/устáть**, it is often used in a past perfective form to indicate a *current* state, i.e. the way one feels *now*. Study the following examples.

Мнé надоéло занимáться.
I am tired/sick of studying.

Нáм надоéло ходи́ть всё врéмя пешкóм.
We are tired of walking everywhere.

Натáше надоéла э́та рабóта.
Natasha is sick of that job.

Им надоéл трéнер по футбóлу.
They are sick of their soccer coach.

4. The construction оди́н из + genitive case

Оди́н из на́ших преподава́телей филатели́ст.

One of our teachers is a stamp collector.

The Russian equivalent for expressing "one of..." is **оди́н (одна́, одно́, одни́) из** + the genitive case. When the person or thing described as "one of" is in a case other than the nominative, only the word **оди́н** (одна́, одно́, одни́) will reflect that case.

— Кто́ э́та де́вушка?   "Who is that young woman?"
— Это одна́ из на́ших студе́нток.   "She's one of our students."

Я всегда́ пла́ваю с одни́м из мои́х друзе́й.
I always swim with one of my friends.

Оле́г попроси́л одного́ из свои́х знако́мых зае́хать за на́ми.
Oleg asked one of his friends to pick us up.

Ната́ша позвони́ла одно́й из свои́х подру́г и пригласи́ла её в го́сти.
Natasha called one of her girlfriends and invited her to come over (to visit).

5. Describing activities and sports events

Са́ша са́м игра́ет в футбо́л и в хокке́й, он стра́стный боле́льщик и хо́дит на все́ ма́тчи, когда́ игра́ют его́ люби́мые кома́нды.

Sasha himself plays soccer and hockey, he is an avid fan and goes to all the games when his favorite teams are playing.

Study the following words and expressions used to describe activities and sports events.

игра́ть (игра́й-) во что́ (+ accusative)	to play something (a game, a sport, etc.)
игра́ть в ша́хматы	to play chess
игра́ть в футбо́л	to play soccer

игра́ть в америка́нский футбо́л	to play football
игра́ть в те́ннис	to play tennis

игра́ть на чём (+ prepositional)	to play an instrument
игра́ть на скри́пке	to play the violin
игра́ть на роя́ле	to play the piano
игра́ть на флейте	to play the flute

игра́ть/сыгра́ть ма́тч	to play a game, a match

прои́грывать/проигра́ть ма́тч со́ счётом X:X	to lose a game with a score of X:X

Кома́нда Теха́сского университе́та проигра́ла ма́тч со счётом 5:2.
The team from Texas University lost the game with a score of 5 to 2.

выи́грывать/вы́играть ма́тч со счётом X:X	to win a game with a score of X:X

На́ша кома́нда вы́играла со счётом 3:0.
Our team won with a score of 3 to 0.

уме́ть игра́ть во что́ (+ accusative)	to know how to, to have the skill to play

Я не уме́ю игра́ть в ша́хматы.
I don't know how to play chess.

боле́ть (боле́й-) за кого́ (+ accusative)	to root for someone

Оле́г боле́ет за кома́нду «Спарта́к».
Oleg is rooting for Spartacus.

Джо́н боле́ет за кома́нду «Янкис».
John is rooting for the Yankees.

болéльщик чегó   an avid fan of

Сáша óчень любит спóрт, он стрáстный болéльщик комáнды «Динáмо».
Sasha really loves sports, he is an avid "Dinamo" fan.

соревновáние по чемý (+ dative)   a competition in
   соревновáние по гимнáстике   gymnastics competition

мáтч по чемý (+ dative)   a game of
   мáтч по волейбóлу   a volleyball game

чемпионáт по чемý (+ dative)   championship in
   чемпионáт по фигýрному катáнию   figure skating championship

счёт X:X   score of X to X
   счёт бы́л 4:2 (read четы́ре двá)   the score was 4 to 2

6. Transitive vs. intransitive reflexive verbs: уви́деть/уви́деться, встрéтить/встрéтиться, познакóмить/познакóмиться

These reflexive verbs imply reciprocal action by the individuals involved. In other words, the reflexive particle **-ся** adds the meaning of "one another."

Мы́ познакóмились в Москвé, когдá мы́ учи́лись в университéте.
We met (one another) in Moscow when we were studying at the university.

По-мóему, мы́ с ни́м гдé-то ви́делись.
It seems to me that he and I have seen each other before.

Ребя́та чáсто встречáются у Иры.
The guys often meet (get together) at Ira's.

When these verbs are used without the particle **-ся**, they are transitive and take a direct object in the accusative case.

Мо́й бра́т познако́мил меня́ со свое́й подру́гой.
My brother introduced me to his girlfriend.

Я о́чень ре́дко ви́жу Ле́ну.
I see Lena very rarely.

Вчера́, когда́ мы́ шли́ на конце́рт, мы́ встре́тили Ната́шу и Ива́на, кото́рые то́же шли́ на конце́рт.
Yesterday when we were on our way to the concert, we met (ran into) Natasha and Ivan, who were also on their way to the concert.

Урóк 10: Мы́ путешéствуем!

1. Multidirectional verbs of motion in the past to indicate round trip

> Джóн éздил на Байкáл, Алан летáл на Урáл.
> John went to Baikal, Alan flew to the Urals.

Recall the use of unprefixed, multidirectional verbs of motion to indicate a round trip in the past tense (*Unit 2*).

— Ты́ не знáешь, кудá éздила Лйнда? "Do you know where Linda went?"
— Онá éздила в Тáллинн. "She went (took a trip) to Tallin."

Моя́ сосéдка по кóмнате éздила в Лóндон в январé.
My roommate went (took a trip) to London in January.

2. По + dative to indicate motion all around

Review that the preposition **по** + the dative case is used to indicate motion throughout or all around a certain place (*Unit 1*). This construction is often used with the verbs **путешéствовать** and **гуля́ть,** and with multi-directional verbs of motion such as **éздить** and **ходи́ть**.

Мы́ путешéствовали по Еврóпе.
We traveled around Europe.

Нáша грýппа путешéствовала по Срéдней Áзии.
Our group traveled around Central Asia.

Вчерá мы́ с брáтом гуля́ли по пáрку.
My brother and I strolled around the park yesterday.

Лйнда и Сáша ходи́ли по Москвé.
Linda and Sasha walked around Moscow.

Мы́ с роди́телями е́здили по все́й Аме́рике.
My parents and I traveled all over America.

3. Short-form adjectives дово́лен (дово́льна, дово́льны) and ви́ден (видна́, ви́дно, видны́)

Review these short-form adjectives from *Unit 7, #8*. They are used throughout *Unit 10* in connection with the theme of traveling.

дово́лен, дово́льна, дово́льны (че́м): to be pleased or satisfied with

Ли́нда о́чень дово́льна свое́й пое́здкой.
Linda is very satisfied with her trip.

ви́ден, видна́, ви́дно, видны́:   to be visible[1]

За э́тими сте́нами видны́ бе́лые пра́здничные собо́ры.
White festive cathedrals are visible beyond these walls.

С моста́ ви́ден ве́сь Петербу́рг.
All of Petersburg is visible from the bridge.

4. Expressing one's impressions

In *Unit 10,* you will be giving your impressions and assessments of places and events. The following sentences use a variety of words and phrases to express general impressions.

The perfective verb **понра́виться** is used in an impersonal construction to indicate an overall assessment. Throughout *Russian Stage 2*, you have used impersonal constructions to provide general impressions of a whole situation (see *Unit 1, Unit 8*). Recall that in impersonal constructions, there is no grammatical subject in the nominative case, and the verb (if there is one) is in the neuter singular. Study the following examples, noting how the English equivalents use "it" in place of the missing Russian subject.

---

[1] Note that the colloquial rendering of this in English is "you can see it" rather than "it is visible."

| — Ка́к ва́м понра́вилось та́м? | "How did you like it there?" |
| | ("How was it?") |

| — Ка́к ва́м понра́вилось в Еги́пте? | "How did you like it in Egypt?" |
| — Та́м замеча́тельно. | "It is marvelous there." |

— Ва́м понра́вилось в Петербу́рге?	"Did you like it in Petersburg?"
— Да́, о́чень. Бы́ло прекра́сно. Мне́	"Yes, very much. It was wonderful."
осо́бенно понра́вились бе́лые но́чи.	I especially liked the white nights."

Бо́льше всего́ can be used to ask or state what one likes "best of all."

— Что́ тебе́ бо́льше всего́ понра́вилось в Петербу́рге?
"What did you like best in Petersburg?"
— Мне́ бо́льше всего́ понра́вились музе́и.
"I liked the museums best."

A superlative formed with a neuter singular adjective, such as **са́мое замеча́тельное,** is used in an equational sentence to say "the very best (thing) is/was...." This superlative remains neuter regardless of the gender or number of the noun completing the equational sentence.

Там всё бы́ло замеча́тельно. Но са́мое замеча́тельное — э́то океа́н.
Everything was marvelous there. But the most marvelous thing is (was) the ocean.

Са́мое интере́сное — э́то монасты́рь.
The most interesting (thing) is the monastery.

Са́мое чуде́сное в Колора́до — э́то го́ры.
The most wondrous thing in Colorodo is the mountains.

5. Means of transportation

The means or vehicle of transportation can be indicated by using the preposition **на +** prepositional or, in some cases, by the instrumental case.

До Арха́нгельска мы́ е́хали по́ездом, от Арха́нгельска на Солове́цкие острова́ мы́ лете́ли на ма́леньком самолёте.
We went by train as far as Arkhangelsk, from Arkhangelsk to the Solovetsky Islands we went by small airplane.

За́втра мы́ уезжа́ем в Бо́стон, мы́ е́дем по́ездом.
We are leaving for Boston tomorrow, we are going by train.

Ле́том мы́ пое́дем на Чёрное мо́ре. Мы́ хоти́м пое́хать на маши́не.
In the summer we are going to the Black Sea. We want to (go by car).

6. Prefixes с-, по-, and про-, and multi-directional verbs of motion

In *Unit 10*, there are three cases where non-spatial prefixes are added to multi-directional verbs of motion, forming a perfective: **сходи́ть, походи́ть, проходи́ть**. Unlike the usual spatial prefixes added to both multi- and uni-directional verbs of motion to form a new aspectual pair, these verbs have only the following forms, in which only the perfective is prefixed.

A. The prefix с- and round trips in the past or future

Бре́нда съе́здила в Петербу́рг.

Мы́ сходи́ли на то́т о́стров, та́м о́чень краси́во.

ходи́ть/сходи́ть   (to go by foot)
е́здить/съе́здить   (to go by vehicle)

You have already seen how the prefix **с-** is added to multi-directional verbs to form a perfective verb indicating a round trip in the past or future (*Unit 7*). Recall that there is no imperfective form with the prefix **c-** in this meaning; also, there is no alternation from **éздить** to **езжáть** in the prefixed form. Further note the hard sign (**ъ**) after the prefix in **съéздить**. In *Unit 10*, the verb **съéздить** occurs frequently in reference to past or future vacation plans. Study the following examples.

> Я давнó хотéл(а) поéхать в Петербýрг, и наконéц, на прóшлой недéле, съéздил(а) тудá.
> I have wanted to go to Petersburg for a long time, and finally I went there (made a trip there) last week.

Recall that in the past tense, the use of this prefixed verb (rather than its unprefixed counterpart) imparts the extra nuance that a specific goal or intention was fulfilled. Don't forget that this is the *only way* to indicate a round trip in the future.

> Когдá вы бýдете в Петербýрге, обязáтельно сходúте в Эрмитáж.
> When you are in Petersburg, make sure you visit the Hermitage.

—Вы не хотúте пойтú в Национáльную галерéю? Сегóдня открылась выставка Пикáссо.	"Would you like to go to the National Gallery? A Picasso exhibit opened there today.
—Хочý. Давáйте схóдим зáвтра.	"I would like to. Let's go tomorrow."

B. The prefix по-: "for a little while"

> Мы немнóго походúли по стáрой чáсти гóрода.
> We walked around the old part of the city for a little while.

The prefix **по-** is added to multi-directional verbs of motion (**ходúть, éздить, бéгать,** and others), to form a perfective verb indicating that the action is limited in time. Note that the multi-directional nature of the action is preserved.

походи́ть = to walk around for a little while
пое́здить = to ride/drive around for a little while
побе́гать = to run/jog for a little while
попла́вать = to swim for a little while

You may have encountered this prefix, with the same function of limiting an action in time, with other verbs as well.

почита́ть = to read for a little while
погуля́ть = to walk/stroll around for a little while
посиде́ть = to sit for a little while
поспа́ть = to sleep for a little while

C. The prefix про-: "for a long while"

Мы́ весь де́нь проходи́ли по ста́рой ча́сти го́рода.
We wandered around the old part of the city for the whole day (all day long).

The prefix **про-** is added to multi-directional verbs of motion to form a perfective verb with a temporal meaning: that the action was prolonged, or the motion took place over an extended period of time. Most often the period of time over which the motion occurs is indicated (in the accusative case with no preposition), emphasizing the lengthiness of the action (e.g. **ве́сь де́нь, це́лый ча́с.**)

Де́ти пробе́гали всё у́тро в па́рке.
The children ran around all morning in the park.

Мы́ прое́здили це́лых пя́ть часо́в по го́роду.
We drove around the city for five whole hours.

7. Verbal adverbs (gerunds)

You have already seen how participles and participle constructions, like the relative clauses into which they can be extended, qualify nouns and agree with these nouns (their antecedents) in gender, number, and case. We shall now consider clauses that modify verbs; that is, specify the manner, the time, or the reason for the action expressed by the main verb in the sentence, or the condition indispensable for its fulfillment. Such clauses are called adverbial clauses and may use verbal adverbs. As with verbal adjectives, *verbal adverbs are intended for passive recognition at this stage of study.* You should be able to recognize them and expand them into a clause, but you are not expected to be able to form them[1].

A verbal adverb can replace a subordinate clause of manner (how), cause (why), condition (if), or time (when). The subject of the verbal adverb is always the same as that of the main verb of the sentence or clause in which it stands. Since they are by definition adverbs, verbal adverbs, unlike verbal adjectives (participles), have no gender, number, person, or case. In addition, verbal adverbs do not have tense.

There are only two kinds of verbal adverbs:

> *Imperfective verbal adverbs* formed from imperfective verbs. They indicate that the action of the verbal adverb takes place simultaneously with the action of the main verb.

> *Perfective verbal adverbs* formed from perfective verbs. They indicate that their action precedes that of the main verb.

A. Formation and usage of verbal adverbs

Verbal adverbs are formed by adding the following suffixes to the verb stem.

Imperfective: **-а/-я**
Perfective: **-в** or **-вши** (obligatory for perfective verbs with the particle **-ся**)

---

[1] See *Appendix XIV* for a summary of the formation rules for verbal adverbs.

Imperfective Verbal Adverbs

Infinitive	Stem	Verbal Adverb
чита́ть	чита́й-	чита́я
жи́ть	жи́в-	живя́
нести́	нёс-	неся́
возвраща́ться	возвраща́й—ся	возвраща́ясь
учи́ться	учи́—ся	уча́сь
бра́ть	б/ра-	беря́
дава́ть	дава́й-	дава́я (-авай- remains before the -я suffix)
говори́ть	говори́-	говоря́
спеши́ть	спеши́-	спеша́

Imperfective verbal adverbs are always stressed on the **-а/-я** ending, unless the verb has stress fixed on the root.

Certain classes of verbs do not form imperfective verbal adverbs:

- stems in **г/к** (пе́чь, бере́чь)
- stems in **-ну** (кивну́ть)
- certain stems in **-а** (жда́ть, ре́зать) Stems in **-я** like смея́-ся and надея́-ся and stems in б/ра- do form verbal adverbs
- certain irregular verbs, including **е́хать, спа́ть, пе́ть, хоте́ть, мо́чь, ле́чь**

Note that the verbal adverb of **бы́ть** is **бу́дучи**.

Study the following examples, noting that imperfective verbal adverbs indicate action simultaneous with that of the main verb.

Расска́зывая о свое́й семье́, Оля всё вре́мя улыба́ется.
When telling about her family, Olya smiles the entire time.

Собира́я свои́ ве́щи, мы нашли́ тво́й купа́льник.
While we were packing our things, we found your bathing suit.

Покупа́я биле́ты, Джо́н познако́милась с Ле́ной.
John met Lena while buying the tickets.

Perfective Verbal Adverbs

Infinitive	Stem	Verbal Adverb
нарисова́ть	нарисова́-	нарисова́в
посмотре́ть	посмотре́-	посмотре́в
отве́тить	отве́ти-	отве́тив
прочита́ть	прочита́й-	прочита́в
откры́ть	откро́й-	откры́в
встре́титься	встрети- ˣ -ся	встре́тившись
верну́ться	верну́- -ся	верну́вшись

Perfective verbal adverbs are always stressed on the syllable immediately before the ending, unless the verb has fixed stress on the root.

Some perfective verbal adverbs are formed by adding the suffix **-я** rather than **-в(ши)** to the stem. This occurs in non-suffixed obstruent stems, in the perfective verbs formed by adding a prefix to **-йти,** and with some suffixed stems in **-и** that also have **-ся.**

Infinitive	Stem	Verbal Adverb
перевести́	переве́д-	переведя́
принести́	принёс-	принеся́
возврати́ться	возврати- ˣ -ся	возвратя́сь
войти́	войти́	войдя́
отойти́	отойти́	отойдя́

Study the following examples, noting how perfective verbal adverbs indicate that the action of verbal adverb precedes the action of the main verb.

Собра́в свои́ ве́щи, мы́ пое́хали на вокза́л.
Having packed our things, we set off for the station.

Прочита́в путеводи́тель, они́ реши́ли пое́хать в музе́й деревя́нной архитекту́ры.
Having read the guidebook, they decided to go to the museum of wooden architecture.

Купи́в биле́ты, Джо́н позвони́л мне́ и пригласи́л меня́ на концéрт.
Having bought the tickets, John called me and invited me to the concert.

B. Special cases

There are some set phrases that do not always follow the restrictions normally imposed on verbal adverbs. The following parenthetic phrases may be used regardless of the predicate verb or its subject. They are some of the most common ones in conversational Russian.

Че́стно говоря́,....	To tell you the truth,....
Вообще́ говоря́,....	Speaking in general,....
Коро́че говоря́,....	In short,....
Ина́че говоря́,....	In other words,....
Ме́жду на́ми говоря́,....	Just between you and me,....